ELIZABETH COLEMAN first came to attention with her wonderfully dark comedy *It's My Party (And I'll Die If I Want To)* which premiered at the 1993 Melbourne Comedy Festival. Its success was eclipsed with the arrival of *Secret Bridesmaids' Business* in 1999 which broke box office records in Melbourne before embarking on a triumphant national tour in 2000. It was adapted for television and screened in 2002. *This Way Up* premiered at Playbox Theatre in 2001. No stranger to the small screen, Coleman's other screenplays for television include *The Secret Life of Us*, *SeaChange*, *Something in the Air*, *Police Rescue* and *The Flying Doctors*.

Secret Bridesmaids' Business

It's My Party (And I'll Die If I Want To)

Two plays by
Elizabeth Coleman

Currency Press,
Sydney

First published in 2003 by
Currency Press Pty Ltd,
PO Box 2287, Strawberry Hills NSW 2012

Secret Bridesmaids' Business was first published by Currency Press, in association with Playbox Theatre in 1999. *It's My Party (And I'll Die If I Want To)* was first published in *The La Mama Collection* by Currency Press in 1997.

Copyright © Elizabeth Coleman, *Secret Bridesmaids' Business* 2003, *It's My Party (And I'll Die If I Want To)* 1993

COPYING FOR EDUCATIONAL PURPOSES

The Australian *Copyright Act 1968* (Act) allows a maximum of one chapter or 10% of this book, whichever is the greater, to be copied by any educational institution for its educational purposes provided that that educational institution (or the body that administers it) has given a remuneration notice to Copyright Agency Limited (CAL) under the Act.

For details of the CAL licence for educational institutions contact CAL, 19/157 Liverpool Street, Sydney, NSW, 2000. Tel: (02) 9394 7600; Fax: (02) 9394 7601; E-mail: info@copyright.com.au

COPYING FOR OTHER PURPOSES

Except as permitted under the Act, for example a fair dealing for the purposes of study, research, criticism or review, no part of this book may be reproduced, stored in a retrieval system, or transmitted in any form or by any means without prior written permission. All inquiries should be made to the publisher at the address above.

Any performance or public reading of *Secret Bridesmaids' Business* or *It's My Party (And I'll Die If I Want To)* is forbidden unless a licence has been received from the author or the author's agent. The purchase of this book in no way gives the purchaser the right to perform the plays in public, whether by means of a staged production or a reading. All applications for public performance should be addressed to the author care of Currency Press.

NATIONAL LIBRARY OF AUSTRALIA CIP DATA
Coleman, Elizabeth, 1962–.
    Secret bridesmaids' business; It's my party (and I'll die if I want to): Two plays.
    ISBN 0 86819 701 7.
    I. Coleman, Elizabeth, 1962– It's my party (and I'll die if I want to). II. Title. III. Title: It's my party (and I'll die if I want to).
    A822.3
Cover design by Kate Florance, Currency Press
Printed by Southwood Press, Marrickville

Contents

Secret Bridesmaids' Business   1
It's My Party (And I'll Die If I Want To)   97

Secret Bridesmaids' Business

Secret Bridesmaids' Business was first produced by Playbox Theatre Centre at The C.U.B. Malthouse, Melbourne, on 14 April 1999, with the following cast:

COLLEEN BACON	Joan Sydney
MEG BACON	Ulli Birvé
ANGELA DIXON	Tara Morice
LUCY DEAN	Kate Johnston
NAOMI BARTLETT	Rachael Beck
JAMES DAVIS	Fred Whitlock

Director, Catherine Hill
Designer, Shaun Gurton
Lighting Designer, Andrew Livingston
Executive Director, Aubrey Mellor

CHARACTERS

COLLEEN BACON, 55+, the bride's mother. Flustered, bossy, well-intentioned.
MEG BACON, 33, the bride. Warm, fragile, fun.
ANGELA DIXON, 34, the Matron of Honour. Loyal, giving, occasionally vague.
LUCY DEAN, 34, Bridesmaid. Earthy, impetuous, direct.
NAOMI BARTLETT, 28, a friend. Sexy, self-absorbed, conflicted.
JAMES DAVIS, 35, the bridegroom. Successful, confident, sincere.
HOTEL HOUSEMAID

SETTING

Secret Bridesmaids' Business takes place in a hotel suite in the hours leading up to Meg Bacon's wedding. Meg's gathered together her mum and her bridesmaids for one last night of good old-fashioned girlie fun—well, that's the plan, anyway.

ACT ONE

SCENE ONE

It's early evening. We're in an elegant hotel, around four star standard. The room contains a double bed, a single bed, a table with four chairs, a TV, a sofa, a mirror, a mini-bar. The usual stuff. A muted city view shows through a window. It's dusk.

There is a door leading off, upstage, to the bathroom and another door, stage right, which leads to the connecting bedroom. Another door, stage left, leads out into the hotel corridor. Overnight bags lie around the room, open and partly unpacked.

A covered wedding dress and a covered bridesmaid's dress are hanging in the wardrobe. We can see the flowing folds of a veil hanging beside them.

A dozen yellow roses in a vase and a large roll of silver ribbon sit on the table.

A woman in her mid to late fifties, COLLEEN, *is talking on the phone. She's clearly enjoying her state of flustered agitation.*

COLLEEN: Seventeen vegetarians?! But we've only got sixteen spinach vol-au-vents! Why didn't you—What? An *hour* ago?! Well he'll just have to make do with a stuffed potato. Now, you will let me know if there are any more problems? All right. Bye— [*Calling towards the bathroom without pausing for breath*] Meg! Why didn't you tell me that Naomi Bartlett's boyfriend's a vegetarian?!

MEG: [*off*] What?

COLLEEN: I said why didn't you tell me that Naomi Bartlett's boyfriend is a vegetarian?!

The bathroom door opens and MEG *enters. She's attractive, thirty-three. She has a line of white bleach above her upper lip. As this conversation takes place she walks to the table and picks up the roll of silver ribbon.*

MEG: Naomi hasn't got a boyfriend.
COLLEEN: Well who's this man she's bringing to the wedding then?
MEG: I don't know. I think it's some guy she met at squash.
COLLEEN: *Some guy she met at—?!* So you're telling me that a total stranger is taking up a place that could've gone to your Great Uncle Reg?
MEG: Mum, we've been through this a million times. I haven't seen Uncle Reg since 1987.
COLLEEN: But you've never even met this vegetarian man.
MEG: M-u-u-u-u-m...
COLLEEN: It's all very well for you to take that tone. You're not the one who had to ring Uncle Reg.
MEG: And did Uncle Reg give a rat's arse?
COLLEEN: [*language*] Meg!
MEG: [*overlapping*] Is this the ribbon for the pews?
COLLEEN: Yes, I had to get that one because they'd run out of the—
MEG: [*overlapping*] But it's too thick.
COLLEEN: Too what? Too *thick?*
MEG: Too *wide.* I told you I wanted it fine, remember? This one looks all... chunky.
COLLEEN: They only had twenty-one metres in the width you wanted and I wasn't going to have half the pews with one width and half the pews with another.
MEG: But we could've put the elegant ribbons up the front and the others on the back pews. No-one would've noticed—

> *The door opens and another woman* MEG's *age enters. She's* ANGELA. *She carries a cardboard box that contains place cards for the reception.*

COLLEEN: I'm not having the church look untidy, Meg. There's nothing wrong with this ribbon!
MEG: [*mildly*] All right, okay... [*The place cards*] That them, Ange?
ANGELA: [*nodding*] Yeah. The receptionist put them away and then went off duty. But they found them eventually.

> *She hands the box to* COLLEEN.

COLLEEN: Thank you, Angela. [*As she opens the box*] What do *you* think of that ribbon? It's not too wide to make a nice bow, is it?

MEG: Mum, forget the ribbon. It's fine, really—

But COLLEEN's *already moved on to another disaster.*

COLLEEN: [*interrupting*] We can't use these!
MEG: What?!
COLLEEN: These name cards! They're not folded properly!
ANGELA: What do you mean—?
COLLEEN: [*overlapping*] Well look! [*Holding up some name cards, she reads*] 'Thank you for sharing our special d'. You can't see the rest of the word!
ANGELA: Oh no…
COLLEEN: We're going to have to re-fold them!
MEG: Show me. Oh, they *are* a bit crooked…
COLLEEN: *A bit?!* They're a dog's breakfast! Come and help me fold them—

   COLLEEN *bustles over to the dining table, reveling in this latest crisis.*

Come on. Quickly.
MEG: I was going to have a shower. Can I do that first?
COLLEEN: No. I need you both to help with this. Come on. Now.

   MEG *and* ANGELA *sit at the table with her.* ANGELA's *already started folding.*

MEG: But this means they're going to have two creases, Mum.
COLLEEN: I know. I'm livid!
MEG: But don't you think that'll look a bit tacky?
COLLEEN: It'll look a lot better than the way they are now!
MEG: I don't know. Ange, what do you think—?
COLLEEN: Your father and I didn't pay all that money for crooked name cards. Here, quickly— [*Handing out cards, demonstrating*] Now make sure you join the bottom corners evenly… like that…
ANGELA: [*holding up a perfectly folded card*] Like that, Mrs. Bacon?
COLLEEN: Good. That's it.

   Meg reads a name card aloud, smiling at Angela.

MEG: Ah, John Dixon. Think I know him… Good-looking guy with a gorgeous wife, right?
ANGELA: That's him. Where's he sitting?

MEG: At Table Eleven.
COLLEEN: [*over her*] Table Eleven.
MEG: Yeah, with Louise and Eric and Sue and Jack and Naomi and, ah, her friend...
COLLEEN: See? You don't even know the man's name.

MEG pulls a playful face at her mother. Meanwhile ANGELA *looks at the seating plan.*

ANGELA: Oh, next to Eric. That's good. He likes Eric.
COLLEEN: Are the children staying with John's parents, Angela?
ANGELA: [*nodding*] 'Til Sunday morning...
COLLEEN: All the way 'til Sunday?
ANGELA: Yeah...
MEG: Oh Ange, are you missing them already?
ANGELA: No way!

They all smile.

Not yet, anyway.
MEG: You know, Holly's growing up so quickly...
ANGELA: I know... Scary, isn't it?
MEG: Remember we always used to say that our kids would play together? At this rate yours are going to baby sit mine.
COLLEEN: Still Sweetheart, better late than never.

MEG nods, pleased. She's clearly given this a lot of thought.

MEG: Yeah. If I have one at thirty-four, one at thirty-five and one at thirty-six, I'm still on target for the three and I won't be too incredibly old when they're growing up.
ANGELA: Three in three years?
MEG: Well I'm thirty-three now, so I'm okay for a couple of years, but the risk of complications increases by about a million percent between thirty-five and thirty-seven , so I'm really even pushing it by having one at thirty-six.
ANGELA: Oh, I don't think so. Lots of women have their first baby after thirty-five—
COLLEEN: [*overlapping*] It's nice for children to be close in age, though. They're good company for each other.
MEG: Yeah, and if they're only one class apart at school, they can play together at— [lunchtime.]

ANGELA: [*overlapping*] Meg, how long have you had that bleach on?
MEG: Oh my God. I forgot! My upper lip's going to be red raw! [*Jumping to her feet*] Why didn't you say something, Mum?
COLLEEN: I can't remember *everything*, Meg—

    MEG *hurriedly exits to the bathroom.*

[*Turning to* ANGELA] Which reminds me—what happened with your shoes again?

    ANGELA *looks like she'd rather not discuss this topic. She tries to fob* COLLEEN *off.*

ANGELA: My shoes were fine. Look, this place card's even more crooked than the others—
COLLEEN: [*overlapping*] Oh of course, it was Lucy's. What happened in the end?

    ANGELA *tries to play the whole thing down.*

ANGELA: Well the woman couldn't find the right fabric to cover them because it was coming from Singapore, and so she—
COLLEEN: [*overlapping*] Thailand.
ANGELA: Yeah, that's right. Thailand. And they only had enough fabric for mine, but in the end it was all— [sorted out]
COLLEEN: [*interrupting, alarmed*] They found some though, didn't they? I thought they'd found the fabric.
ANGELA: Yeah they did. And it's almost exactly the same. You know, I can't seem to fold this one properly—
COLLEEN: [*interrupting*] Almost? You mean it's not the same fabric?!
ANGELA: [*oops*] Well, not technically. But it's exactly the same colour.
COLLEEN: [*alarm bells ringing*] It's not shiny, is it?
ANGELA: Well it's just, it's just maybe got the *tiniest hint* of a sheen—
COLLEEN: [*interrupting*] But your shoes have got a matt finish!
ANGELA: Yeah I know, but you can hardly see it—
COLLEEN: [*overlapping*] Why didn't Meg tell me this?!
ANGELA: Ah, I'm not sure that Lucy's mentioned it to her…
COLLEEN: What?!
ANGELA: I don't think she thought it was that important.
COLLEEN: But she's going to be devastated.
ANGELA: It's okay, Mrs. Bacon. They look exactly the same. And besides, people probably won't notice our feet—

COLLEEN: But the dresses are cocktail length!

    ANGELA *is rendered speechless. What can one possibly say in the face of such disaster?*

I told Meg she should have ankle length, but no, they had to be halfway up to your knees. And now this!

ANGELA: I really don't think it's going to matter that much—

    But COLLEEN *is marching over to the bathroom door, calling out briskly.*

COLLEEN: Meg! There's a problem with Lucy's shoes—!

    The bathroom door opens and MEG *re-emerges, bleach removed.*

MEG: Have I got a really obvious blonde moustache now? Sometimes a blonde one's as bad as a dark one—

COLLEEN: [*interrupting, dramatically*] Meg, Lucy's shoes!

MEG: What? What about them?

COLLEEN: The fabric's different to Angela's!

MEG: What do you mean, different?

COLLEEN: It's shiny!

MEG: Shiny?

ANGELA: It's not *that* shiny—

MEG: [*overlapping*] But Angela's shoes are matt!

COLLEEN: *I* know that!

ANGELA: You can hardly see it. Really. If you could notice it, Lucy would have mentioned it.

COLLEEN: This is so typical of Lucy, causing trouble like this.

MEG: M-u-u-u-m… [*Turning to* ANGELA] Can you really not see it?

ANGELA: Really. If I hadn't told you, you probably wouldn't have even noticed.

    At this moment there is a knock at the door.

COLLEEN: Oh, *I* would've noticed.

LUCY: [*calling from outside*] It's me!

MEG: Speak of the devil. [*Calling as she walks to the door*] Are your ears burning, Luce?

    She opens the door. LUCY *enters. She's tall, striking, thirty-four. She carries an overnight bag.*

LUCY: Huh..?

MEG *and* LUCY *squeal in a 'girlie' fashion as they give each other a great big hug. Then—*

[*Entering*] Hi, Angela, Colleen—
COLLEEN: [*overlapping*] Lucy, show me your shoes.
LUCY: What—?
COLLEEN: Can you show me your shoes, please? Quickly.

Misunderstanding her, LUCY *gives her a funny look and holds out her foot.*

No, not those. Your bridesmaid's shoes.
LUCY: Oh, right—
MEG: Mum, how about saying hello?
COLLEEN: I'm sorry. Hello Lucy. Angela tells me your shoes are shiny.

LUCY *gets them out of her bag, throwing a* 'thanks a lot' *look at* ANGELA.

ANGELA: That's not exactly what I said—
LUCY: They're not *very* shiny—
MEG: Why didn't you tell me?
LUCY: Because you can't even notice the difference.
COLLEEN: Well I certainly hope you're right.
ANGELA: She is, really.
COLLEEN: Can you get me one of your shoes, Angela?

As ANGELA *walks at a normal pace,* COLLEEN *barks at her:*

Quickly!

ANGELA *reluctantly hurries to the wardrobe and grabs a shoe. She brings it back to* COLLEEN. *Meanwhile* COLLEEN *and* MEG *peer at* LUCY*'s shoe under a desk light.*

It's definitely shiny!
LUCY: You can hardly notice.
MEG: You can notice *a bit*...

LUCY *looks like she's trying to contain deep tension.*

COLLEEN: [*grabbing* ANGELA*'s shoe*] Here, let me see—
ANGELA: See? They're no different—

COLLEEN *holds up both shoes. They all peer at them as she gasps in horror.*

COLLEEN: They're chalk and cheese!
LUCY: Oh, they are not!
COLLEEN: Look at them! They don't match at all!
LUCY: [*spontaneous outburst*] Oh, what a load of crap!
MEG: Lucy! She didn't mean that, Mum. She's just a bit—
LUCY: [*interrupting*] Sorry. Sorry, Colleen. I got caught in traffic. I'm stressed out. Sorry.
COLLEEN: That's all right...

> *The younger women exchange glances as* COLLEEN *makes the most of her martyrdom.*

I just want everything to be nice for Meg, and I'm sorry if that upsets some people...
MEG: Mum... it doesn't. And everything's going to be perfect... [*To* ANGELA *and* LUCY] Isn't it?
ANGELA: Of course. It'll be a beautiful wedding, Mrs. Bacon.

> *They turn to look at* LUCY *expectantly: Your turn. She obliges.*

LUCY: Yeah. It'll be great. And you really shouldn't worry about the shoes. No-one who matters will take any notice.
COLLEEN: Well *I* took notice, but never mind...

> LUCY *bites back a response as* ANGELA *jumps in quickly to ease the tension.*

ANGELA: Lucy, we're re-folding the name cards. Here, come and help—

> *She sits at the table.* LUCY *sits too.*

LUCY: So, what are we doing—?

> *But before* ANGELA *can demonstrate,* COLLEEN *grabs the place cards from her hands.*

COLLEEN: Actually Angela, I think I'll finish folding them in my room...
MEG: Are you okay, Mum?
LUCY: [*through gritted teeth*] Sorry, Colleen.
COLLEEN: [*ignoring* LUCY] I'm fine, Sweetheart. I just need some peace and quiet for a few minutes. Excuse me...

> *Martyrdom in full flight, she exits into the other bedroom.*

LUCY: Sorry, Meg. I didn't know it was such a big deal— [*Turning straight to* ANGELA] Why'd you tell her they were shiny—?
ANGELA: [*overlapping*] I didn't. Well, I didn't mean to—

MEG: [*suddenly interrupting*] Hey, where's your dress?
LUCY: In the car.
MEG: In the car?! What if someone steals it?!
LUCY: No-one's going to steal a fifteen year old Corolla.
MEG: I meant the dress!
LUCY: Okay. I'll go get it now. Angela, want to come with me?
ANGELA: [*surprised*] Me?
LUCY: Yeah. There's other stuff to carry too.
MEG: Where are you parked?
LUCY: Downstairs. In the basement.
MEG: [*with relief*] Oh…
LUCY: [*over her, to* ANGELA] Come on—
MEG: I'll come too.
LUCY: [*a little too quickly*] No, I just need Angela.

> MEG *and* ANGELA *look at her in surprise.*

Come on, Angela.
MEG: [*grinning*] Oh, I get it. This is Secret Bridesmaids' Business.
LUCY: [*smiling*] Yeah.
ANGELA: [*first she's heard of it*] Oh, okay! Well why don't you have that shower you were wanting and keep out of our— [way.]

> *A knock at the door.*

MEG: Who's that?

> MEG *answers it to a* HOTEL HOUSEMAID. *She's holding a bridesmaid's dress.*

Oh, hi…
HOUSEMAID: Is Miss Dean in here?
LUCY: Yeah, that's me.
HOUSEMAID: I hope it's all right, but you left your car door unlocked. We've had a few thefts lately, so I took this out for you. I hope you don't mind—
LUCY: [*grabbing it*] Yes I *do* mind! What if *I* wanted to go down and get it?!
ANGELA: Lucy!
MEG: No, that's nice of you. Thank you.
HOUSEMAID: I'm sorry if I shouldn't have—I didn't mean to upset anyone—

MEG: [*overlapping*] No, don't take any notice of her. Thanks a lot.
LUCY: [*approaching her*] Sorry—

> *The* HOUSEMAID *sees* LUCY *coming and virtually breaks into a run as she exits.*

[*Calling to the closed door*] Sorry.
MEG: Is there anyone else you'd like to offend while you're at it?
LUCY: Yeah, you. Have a shower. You stink.
MEG: [*sniffing her underarm*] I do not stink. Why don't you just say—'Get lost. We want to talk Secret Bridesmaids' Business'.
LUCY: Get lost. We want to talk Secret Bridesmaids' Business.

> MEG *starts walking towards the bathroom.*

MEG: Fine—but just remember—if anyone ties inflated condoms to the front of James' car, they die.

> *And with a grin she exits into the bathroom, closing the door behind her.*
>
> LUCY *watches the door, waiting for it to close, then guides* ANGELA *to the far side of the room.* ANGELA's *all smiles, anticipating a fun bridesmaids' secret.*

ANGELA: [*chirpily*] I didn't know we had Secret Bridesmaids' Business!
LUCY: [*overlapping, urgent, low*] Angela, listen to me—I think James has been having an affair.
ANGELA: [*loudly*] What?! [*Lowering her voice*] What did you say?
LUCY: I said James has been having an affair.

> ANGELA *is totally gobsmacked as the bathroom door opens and* MEG *re-emerges.*

MEG: It might help if I took my girlie stuff with me…

> *She picks up her toiletries bag.* ANGELA *and* LUCY *smile at her in a really false, strangled kind of manner.* MEG's *amused.*

God. You two are so bad at acting like you haven't got a secret. And confetti's out too. I don't want rainbow-coloured stains on my wedding dress.

> *She walks back into the bathroom and closes the door.*

ANGELA: [*low*] You must have it wrong.
LUCY: [*low*] No I haven't. He's been fucking Naomi Bartlett!

ANGELA: Naomi Bartlett?!

    LUCY *nods.*

No way! She's a friend of Meg's—
LUCY: Huh. Meg *thinks* she is.

    Then, suddenly, from the bathroom—

MEG: Well *that's* just great!

    LUCY *and* ANGELA *look startled: Did* MEG *hear? The bathroom door opens again and* MEG *re-emerges. But her tone is playful.*

I forgot to bring my loofah!
LUCY: Huh—?
MEG: Did you two bring a loofah?
ANGELA: What?
MEG: A loofah. Have you got one?
LUCY: Who packs a loofah when they're only away for one night?
MEG: I'll take that as a no. Ange, you?
ANGELA: [*shaking her head*] Sorry.
MEG: [*joking*] Great. So how am I supposed to scrape the dead skin cells off my thighs?
LUCY: I could ring downstairs and get a cheese grater.

    ANGELA *tries to laugh, but it comes out sounding forced and a little strangled.*

MEG: You right there, Ange, or are you choking on something?
LUCY: Just rack off and have your shower. [*Playfully pushing her*] Go on.
MEG: All right, all right... I'm going.

    MEG *grins and exits into the bathroom.*

ANGELA: [*low*] Where did you hear this?!
LUCY: Naomi's sister-in-law is best friends with Carol at work, and we were reading this article about infidelity in *Marie Claire* this arvo, and Carol tells me that her best friend's sister-in-law has been sleeping with a guy who's engaged—she didn't know that I knew Naomi—
ANGELA: [*overlapping*] But she could have lots of sisters-in-law—
LUCY: [*overlapping*] But she said Naomi's name—
ANGELA: [*overlapping*] Yeah, but, James isn't the only guy who's engaged—

LUCY: [*overlapping*] She said James' name too!
ANGELA: [*overlapping*] His surname?
LUCY: No, but—
ANGELA: [*interrupting*] Well there you go. James is a pretty common name.
LUCY: Yeah but Naomi told her sister-in-law that this guy is engaged to a *friend* of hers!

> This does make things look pretty incriminating, but ANGELA *is desperate not to believe it.*

ANGELA: [*shaking her head*] No way… it must be somebody else…
LUCY: Who else could it be? And Carol reckons it went on for four months.
ANGELA: Four months?!
LUCY: Yeah. And it only ended two weeks ago!
ANGELA: Oh, it couldn't be him—
LUCY: [*interrupting*] But Naomi rang her sister-in-law on Tuesday, and she was crying because he's getting married this Saturday morning—*tomorrow!!*

> *The sound of a toilet flushing can be heard. They both look towards the bathroom warily, then lower their voices yet again.*

ANGELA: No, no way… Carol must have made a mistake…
LUCY: I don't see how—but she's going to talk to her friend tonight and try and find out this James guy's surname—
ANGELA: Who is? Carol?
LUCY: Yeah. And then she's going to ring me—
ANGELA: [*interrupting*] And what's she going to do?
LUCY: [*impatiently*] Just let me tell you! She's going to find out this guy's surname, and then she's going to ring me here on the mobile.
ANGELA: [*with mixed feelings*] Here?
LUCY: But she's tried to get hold of her friend a few times already and she hasn't been home, so let's just hope she comes back—because I'd rather tell Meg it's definitely him than just say it's a guy called James.
ANGELA: What?

> LUCY *registers the unspoken objection. Her response is very definite—no greys.*

LUCY: Well we'll have to tell her, either way.

ANGELA is absorbing all this as the bathroom door re-opens and MEG emerges in a hotel bathrobe. She grins as she walks to the bed.

MEG: So, have you sorted out the Secret Bridesmaids' Business?
LUCY/ANGELA: Yeah/Yep...
MEG: Great. I'll expect a huge surprise, then.

Totally unaware of the irony, she picks up a white towel from the bed and playfully puts it on her head like a veil, doing a deliberately silly song and dance routine as she heads back into the bathroom.

We're going to the chapel and—We're going to get ma-a-a-rried—Going to the chapel of love...!
LUCY: [*making a strained joke*] Don't give up your day job.

MEG grins at them, then wanders back into the bathroom and closes the door. The sound of the shower is heard throughout the following conversation.

ANGELA: We can't tell her, Lucy.
LUCY: [*flummoxed*] What?!
ANGELA: We can't tell her.
LUCY: [*looking at ANGELA like she's a moron*] We *have* to tell her.
ANGELA: But Meg's been waiting her whole life for this day. We can't ruin it for her—
LUCY: James has done that, not us.
ANGELA: Has he? We don't know for certain, Lucy—
LUCY: Oh, come on. A guy called James who's getting married tomorrow to a friend of Naomi's—?
ANGELA: Well, Naomi's probably got lots of friends—
LUCY: Oh, give me a break—
ANGELA: We can't do this to her—!
LUCY: [*overlapping, exasperated*] But she needs to know!
ANGELA: But what if she already does?
LUCY: Oh, what?!
ANGELA: Well maybe James has told her everything—that's if there's anything to tell—Maybe they've already sorted it out?
LUCY: No way. She would have told me.

ANGELA: Not necessarily. She wouldn't want you to think that James was a bastard.

LUCY: Huh. Too late for that.

ANGELA: Look, Lucy, I just don't think we've got the right to—

LUCY: [*interrupting, patronising*] Don't you think Meg's got the right to make an informed decision?

ANGELA: Maybe she already is.

LUCY: *Or*—maybe she's under the mistaken impression that she can trust the guy she's marrying?!

ANGELA *takes a beat or two to muster her argument.*

ANGELA: Look, Lucy, I know you've been Meg's best friend since uni, but I've known her since we were *seven* and—

LUCY: [*overlapping*] Oh, we're not playing 'Who knows Meg the best', are we?

ANGELA: No, I'm just saying that ever since we were kids her wedding day's been her dream—she used to get in trouble for doodling designs of her wedding dress instead of doing her long division—!

LUCY: So—?!

ANGELA: And she's had navy picked out as her bridesmaids' colour since we saw *Ice Castles* in 1980!

LUCY: *So?!*

ANGELA: And when Paul left and she hit thirty she thought it'd never happen, but now it finally has—

LUCY: Jesus. This has got nothing to do with anything—

ANGELA: Lucy, she's got a three thousand dollar engagement ring, a two thousand dollar wedding dress, one hundred people coming at eighty dollars a head, cousins here from New Zealand, flowers and outfits and hire cars—not to mention a honeymoon in Paris and Venice—do you want to spoil all that for her too?

LUCY: See, this is the problem when everyone puts all their emotional energy into *one day*. It's just one day, for God's sake. And because of one dumb party being ruined, you're prepared to let her have a lifetime of misery.

ANGELA: Who are *you* to say she'll have a 'lifetime of misery'? You're not her.

LUCY: I'm not saying I am her—

ANGELA: And *you* might think it's just some 'dumb party' but this is the

most important day of Meg's life. And just because *you* think it's stupid or sexist or something—
LUCY: I didn't say that—
ANGELA: [*overlapping*] And what about kids? You know how much Meg wants a big family. This could be her last chance.
LUCY: So you want her to have kids with the wrong guy?
ANGELA: I don't think it's our place to say he *is* the wrong guy.

> LUCY *snorts in disbelief again, then she takes a few deep breaths and tries another tack.*

LUCY: [*patronising*] Look, Angela, you're lucky. You met John when you were young and you've always been happy. But things aren't that simple for everyone—
ANGELA: [*overlapping*] Oh, please—
LUCY: [*overlapping*] I'm just saying, if a person's life has always gone smoothly, sometimes they don't understand how complicated things can get for—
ANGELA: [*overlapping angrily*] Yes that's me, Lucy. I'm an old married woman, and my life is totally boring.
LUCY: I didn't say that.
ANGELA: But that's what you think.
LUCY: No it's not—
ANGELA: [*overlapping*] Don't insult me, Lucy. I know you think that.
LUCY: [*only half telling the truth*] No I don't.
ANGELA: [*only saying this because she's been pushed*] And why are you so keen to ruin Meg's wedding anyway? I reckon you're just *jealous.*
LUCY: Jealous?!
ANGELA: Well *you* met James first—
LUCY: So? What's that got to do with anything—?
ANGELA: [*overlapping*] And you liked him—
LUCY: Oh, for *two* weeks, *two years ago!*
ANGELA: [*not really believing this*] Maybe you still do.
LUCY: So *I* want Meg to break up with James so *I* can have him?
ANGELA: [*sighing*] No, of course not, that's not what I'm saying. Look, I just meant—I don't know what I meant—I—
LUCY: [*interrupting*] I'm not the one who's been fucking the guy!

> *They hear the shower been turned off.*

They both turn to look towards the bathroom, registering the sudden silence. They stare at each other angrily for a moment, then collect themselves and lower their voices...

ANGELA: Look, I'm sorry Lucy, I didn't mean that, I'm sorry, but I just don't think we should... Look, can we agree to wait until Carol rings and we find out the guy's surname? Please?

LUCY thinks for a moment. This is a patently reasonable suggestion.

LUCY: But I'm not even sure that she'll definitely ring.

ANGELA: Well, can we put a time on it, then? Can we say that if Carol hasn't rung by—I don't know—ten thirty, we'll talk about it again?

Again LUCY can't deny that this is a reasonable suggestion.

[*Pressing her advantage*] Wouldn't you rather know it's definitely him?

LUCY: [*after a beat*] All right. What time is it now?

ANGELA: [*looking at her watch*] Quarter to eight.

LUCY: Quarter to eight. Okay, we'll give it 'til ten thirty, and if Carol hasn't rung, we'll re-assess.

ANGELA: So you promise you won't say anything to Meg until we've talked about it again?

LUCY: [*Petulantly*] I promise.

ANGELA: Good.

LUCY and ANGELA stare at each other, at an impasse. The argument resolved (for now), they're back to where they've always been; two women with nothing in common save their friendship with Meg.

They smile at each other awkwardly, not sure how to bridge the silence. Then ANGELA spots one of the offending bridesmaids' shoes on a table, picks it up and exits into the other room.

LUCY watches her go, then childishly blows a raspberry and gives 'the finger' to the closed door. Then gradually... she seems to notice the audience. The fourth wall slides away and the lighting state fades to be replaced by a spotlight, as we move into...

SCENE TWO

Spotlight on LUCY. *She meets the audience's collective eyes, staring out at them a little defensively, then speaks.*

LUCY: Go on, look at me like that if you want, but I'm just trying to be a good friend here. It's not like I'm *enjoying* this—it's not like I'm rubbing my hands together with glee, going 'Great, a chance to chuck Meg's heart in a blender!' Hardly... [*Pauses*] I can think of a lot more fun ways to spend a day, believe me—but real friends *tell the truth.* End of story. And it's all very well to hide behind niceness and lame excuses, but—oh look, maybe that's not fair. Stuff it, I don't care—Angela's another one who's got this whole wedding thing way out of whack... [*Frustration tempered by amusement*] If you ask me—and I know you didn't—weddings suck. And I'll tell you why. Because they force decent people to lie. I mean, who can *honestly* say to another person 'Yes, I know *for certain* that I'll forsake all others for the rest of my life?' [*She gives a little laugh. What a ridiculous notion*] No-one, that's who. If you ask me, the vows should go 'Right now I feel like forsaking all others, but let's consult again further down the track...' [*Amused for a moment, then she remembers the situation, and her anger returns*] Jesus, if I saw James right now... Why ask Meg to marry him if he can't even keep his dick in his pants while they're *engaged..?* [*She meets the audience's collective eyes*] Oh yeah yeah, I know what you're thinking. Some couples *can* be happy forever. Well, they've won life's lottery. Half their luck. But the rest of us have to keep buying tickets...

And buying, and buying, and buying... Sometimes *I* feel like I'm running out of raffle books... Jesus, men have done terrible things to me, but I've done awful stuff to them too. I've been unfaithful to boyfriends on [*Thinks*] three... [*Thinks again*] no, technically four occasions, and I'm not proud of that. But you know what else? I have *never* been unfaithful to a *friend.* Because friendship's too important to stuff around with. So, all right—I can wait 'til Carol rings, and I can cross all my fingers and toes that it isn't the same James, but if it *is...* I've never kept a friend in the dark—and wedding or no wedding, I'm not about to start.

Fade to black.

SCENE THREE

Lights up. MEG *has emerged fresh from her shower. She's wrapped in a fluffy white towel and carries a bottle of expensive body lotion.*

ANGELA *is so eager to hide her tension that she shows a ridiculous amount of interest in* MEG*'s shower.*

ANGELA: Here she is! How was your shower? Hot enough for you?
MEG: Yeah, it was fine—
ANGELA: [*right over the top of her*] Good water pressure?
MEG: Huh—?
ANGELA: Was it good water pressure?
MEG: [*bemusedly*] Yeah it was okay—
ANGELA: Did you manage all right without the loofah?
MEG: What? Yeah—
ANGELA: [*overlapping, pointing to her dry hair*] And you didn't wash your hair?
MEG: My shower's not really that interesting, Ange. You need to get out more.

    LUCY *re-enters, trying to mask her tension with joviality.*

LUCY: Hey, let's raid the mini-bar!
ANGELA: Great idea!
MEG: [*puzzled*] You don't drink.
ANGELA: Oh yeah. I forgot.

    MEG *gives her a funny look, then turns back to* LUCY.

MEG: Mum bought some champagne. It's in the fridge.
LUCY: [*opening the fridge*] Wooh. Four bottles.

    LUCY *busies herself getting out a champagne bottle, which she promptly drops.*

LUCY: Ooops! Shit!
MEG: You're not getting nervous on me, are you Luce?
LUCY: [*a handy excuse*] I might be.
MEG: You big wuss-bag. If anyone should be getting jittery around here, it's *me*.
ANGELA: [*hastily, with significance*] Why? What's the matter? Are you worried about something?!

MEG *gives her a look: That was strange reaction to a throwaway comment.*

MEG: No.

ANGELA *can't take the tension anymore. She's got to get out of there.*

ANGELA: I think *I'll* have a shower now.

LUCY: Great idea! See you later.

As ANGELA *heads for the bathroom, a barely perceptible look passes between she and* LUCY: Don't even think about it.

ANGELA *exits into the bathroom, closing the door.*

MEG *looks the tiniest bit puzzled, but* LUCY *distracts her with the champagne.*

Stand back, ladies and gentlemen, girls and boys—

MEG: [*overlapping*] Hang on a sec—can you put some of this on my back first?

She hands LUCY *the Chanel body lotion.*

LUCY: Sure.

MEG *turns away from* LUCY. LUCY *starts rubbing the body lotion into her back.*

MEG: Rub it all over, Luce.

As LUCY *rubs in the body lotion her face betrays her tension, but of course* MEG *can't see that.* LUCY*'s an impetuous person and it's a struggle not to blurt out the truth.*

The sound of a shower running comes from the bathroom.

LUCY: Hmm… This stuff stinks.

MEG: It'd want to, for one hundred and thirty-five bucks.

LUCY: One hundred and thirty-five bucks? I've had cars that cost less than that.

MEG: I know. I've had to kickstart them. [*A beat or two of silence, then…*] It's James' favourite… I haven't worn it for a month so he'll forget all about it. Sneaky, huh? And I thought if I put it on tonight and again in the morning it'll seep into all my pores and I'll have this sexy smell that comes from inside me. It'll drive him nuts.

LUCY: Great.

MEG: [*after a beat*] Oh, I know *you* think big weddings are dumb, but I can't wait for the whole thing to— [start]

LUCY: [*interrupting*] Why does everyone think I think big weddings are dumb?

MEG: Because you've said so on at least forty-seven occasions.

LUCY: But that was before I knew you were having one. And anyway, why do you care what I think?

MEG: [*grinning*] I don't. [*Beat*] Oh, I can see it now Luce... We'll arrive at this posh hotel and I'll still be wearing my wedding dress because who wants to take it off before they have to? And the people in the foyer will say *Isn't she beautiful* and *Don't they make a lovely couple?* 'cause we'll have this incredible glow about us—

LUCY: That'll be sweat from all the dancing.

MEG: Probably.

    LUCY *tries to assume a casual, non-committal air.*

LUCY: So listen—how are you feeling about the whole marriage thing?

MEG: Oh, you know me. I'm convinced my hem's going to fall down, or I'll trip over halfway up the aisle, or the disco guy won't turn up or someone will have a fight and the flowers will wilt and the guests will get food poisoning—

LUCY: [*overlapping*] That'll happen for sure, but I meant the bigger picture. You know, like—how are you feeling about the 'til death do you part' thing?

MEG: Great. Fantastic. Aren't the roses gorgeous?

LUCY: Huh?

    MEG *gestures towards the yellow roses on the table.*

MEG: James sent me those. The card said *I will love you always.*

LUCY: Yeah, nice— [*Grinning as a memory occurs*] But you know what yellow roses remind me of—

MEG: [*overlapping, groaning*] I know, I know! Don't say it!

LUCY: Remember when you got me to send you those yellow roses with an anonymous card to make that bastard Gavin jealous—?

MEG: Bevan.

LUCY: What?

MEG: His name was Bevan. And he didn't care less. He asked if he could give them to his mum, remember?

LUCY: [*grinning*] Jesus…

They both shake their heads and laugh, then…

MEG: [*a fond memory*] God he was a prick. I adored him.
LUCY: Of course you did. You had lousy taste in men back then.
MEG: Ha! Look who's talking! What about— [*Stopping as she has a sudden thought*] Oh my God—David! Did David ring?!
LUCY: [*grinning*] We had dinner last night.
MEG: You *had dinner?! Now* she tells me. Why didn't you tell me?
LUCY: You were busy organising something—
MEG: So what happened? Where did you go?
LUCY: Café Di Stasio.
MEG: Nice. Did he pick you up?
LUCY: Yep.

MEG *raises her eyebrows and whistles.*

MEG: Good sign. And what kind of car's he got?
LUCY: A blue one.
MEG: And what did you wear?
LUCY: The maroon crepe top with the black velvet applique—
MEG: The one with the slim-fit sleeves?
LUCY: Yeah.
MEG: I love that. Did you wear the skirt with it?
LUCY: No—the suede-look pants.
MEG: The black ones?
LUCY: Yeah, the ones with the flair below the knee—
MEG: Perfect! They're really slimming—not that you need that. And was it good..? [*Slightly tentative*] Did he talk about Sandra..?
LUCY: Yeah.
MEG: Well? What did he say?
LUCY: He said he's over her—
MEG: [*interrupting*] Fantastic!
LUCY: Yeah, but who knows if it's true.
MEG: Well, what were his exact words?
LUCY: 'I'm over her.'
MEG: Yeah, but did he say I'm *over* her or I'm over *her*?
LUCY: See, this is the thing. I couldn't tell. And I tried to get him to say it again, but he didn't.
MEG: Well, could you talk to him? Was he witty or smart?

LUCY: [*nodding*] Witty *and* smart.
MEG: Interested in your life?
LUCY: Yeah, but they always sound interested in your life before they go to bed with you.
MEG: That's true.

> Then LUCY *grins mischievously.*

LUCY: Mind you, he still sounded interested afterwards.

> MEG *laughs and hits* LUCY *playfully.*

MEG: Ha! You did the deed?! You said you weren't going to do it on the first date anymore.
LUCY: I wasn't going to, but I couldn't help it. When he poured the wine his sleeves rode up, and he had arms like an AFL player—
MEG: [*overlapping*] I knew that, remember? I saw him in a singlet at Safeway that time—
LUCY: God, he's got seriously sexy arms… When he carried me into his room I just—
MEG: He *carried you* into his room—?!
LUCY: [*nodding*] Yeah, and he picked me up like I weighed three ounces.
MEG: Oh my God… and how was the sex? Was it good?
LUCY: Amazing.
MEG: I knew it would be.
LUCY: As soon as he started kissing me I—
MEG: [*overlapping*] Good kisser?
LUCY: [*nodding*] Superb. He holds your face in his hands—
MEG: Oh my God… I *love* that!
LUCY: And that was it. I couldn't stop myself.
MEG: [*admiringly*] It's so great how you can't stop yourself. I've *always* been able to stop myself, no matter how advanced things are.
LUCY: [*grinning*] I wasn't stopping anything.
MEG: So are you going out again?
LUCY: [*shrugging*] He said he'd ring me on Wednesday.
MEG: Well, he'll ring you on Wednesday.
LUCY: No. If he was a *woman* and he said 'I'll ring you on Wednesday', he'd ring me on Wednesday, but he's a man so 'I'll ring you on Wednesday' means 'Maybe I'll ring you sometime if I feel like it'.
MEG: [*laughing*] Yeah, true.

COLLEEN *re-enters with the place card box and an air of practised brightness.*

COLLEEN: Well, I've finished folding the place cards.

MEG: Thanks for doing that, Mum.

COLLEEN: [*holding one out*] See? You can see the whole sentence now.

MEG: Great. See, Lucy?

LUCY *tries to look at the name card like it matters, but* COLLEEN *senses her lack of interest.*

LUCY: Yeah, great.

COLLEEN *snatches the card place card from her and puts it back in its box with pursed lips.* LUCY *gestures to* MEG: *What did I do now?* MEG *jumps in to save things, as usual.*

MEG: We're going to open the champagne, Mum. Do you want a glass?

COLLEEN: Just a splash, Sweetheart. I won't officially break my diet 'til— [tomorrow]

COLLEEN*'s gaze suddenly falls onto the ribbons. She gasps in abject horror.*

Oh no!!! Oh no!!!

MEG: [*alarmed*] What?! What is it?!

COLLEEN: I forgot to bring the tape measure—!

MEG: What?

COLLEEN: [*picking up the ribbon*] For the ribbon—we need to cut it into one metre lengths!

MEG: You said you were going to put it in your bag—

COLLEEN: I forgot! There were so many things to do—!

MEG: Remind me why it has to be exactly one metre, again?

COLLEEN: Because the ends of the pews are twenty-seven centimetres and it has to be long enough to go around them and make a big bow!

MEG: I'll ring Reception and see if they can send a tape measure up—

LUCY: But couldn't you just measure out the length you want—like this— [*She grabs the ribbon and demonstrates*] —and then do the same length again?

A small silence as MEG *and* COLLEEN *realise how incredibly simple it is.*

MEG: [*grinning*] Not just a pretty face.

COLLEEN: Yes, you're right. I suppose we could do that.
> *She makes a real effort to smile at* LUCY *in a friendly fashion.*

Thank you, Lucy.
LUCY: That's okay. And Colleen, I *am* sorry about the shoes—
COLLEEN: It's all right. I might have overreacted—slightly. We've had a lot of last-minute hiccups and I'd just found out that Naomi Bartlett's fellow is a vegetarian—
LUCY: [*overlapping, hopefully*] Naomi Bartlett's got a fellow?!
MEG: No. She's bringing some guy she met at squash.
LUCY: [*deflated*] Oh.
COLLEEN: And Meg's Great Uncle Reg isn't invited. But anyway, we won't get into that...
> *The shower is heard been turned off.*

The important thing is that we're all here together, celebrating Meg's special day.
MEG: Oh, Mum... let's just get into that champers, eh?
LUCY: Stand back!
> LUCY *pops the cork. They make ad-lib reactions: 'Wooh!', 'Quick quick!', 'It's all fizzy!', etc.* COLLEEN *and* MEG *quickly grab champagne glasses to catch the bubbles. Ad-lib laughter etc. as required.*

Got it?
MEG: Got it!
> *As* LUCY *pours the champagne into the glasses,* ANGELA *re-enters from the bathroom wearing a silky nightie. She looks fresh and cleansed, and she's had time to reconstruct her air of calm. Her wet hair is wrapped in a towel.*

COLLEEN: Oh Angela, you're just in time for a glass of champagne.
MEG: She doesn't drink, Mum.
COLLEEN: Oh of course. I knew that.
MEG: There's lemonade and orange juice in the fridge, Ange.
ANGELA: Actually I'm more hungry than thirsty. Is anyone else hungry?
LUCY: Yeah I'm starving.
COLLEEN: [*nodding*] I'm a bit hungry.
MEG: Oh, I'm sorry. I didn't even *think* about dinner.

COLLEEN: Well you've had a lot of other things on your mind, Sweetheart.

Lucy's mobile phone starts ringing.

LUCY *and* ANGELA *dart a startled look at one another.*

LUCY: Oooh! Oh, that's my mobile!

ANGELA: [*over her, startled*] That's your phone!

As LUCY *gets her mobile out of her bag,* MEG *shakes her head in bemusement...*

MEG: Your nerves are shot to pieces, Luce. [*Turning to* ANGELA] Hey, why don't we get a pizza?

ANGELA: [*pre-occupied by* LUCY*'s phone call*] What?

LUCY: [*into phone*] Hello?

MEG: A pizza.

ANGELA: [*distracted*] Yeah, pizza would be nice.

LUCY: [*into phone*] Oh. No. Everything's fine. No thank you. I'm fine. Goodbye.

She hangs up. They're all staring at her, especially ANGELA.

LUCY: It was Telstra. Am I happy with my mobile service?

MEG: God. How rude to ring on a Friday night. Is pizza okay with you, Mum?

COLLEEN: Fine. As long as it's low-fat cheese.

ANGELA: But no anchovies.

The telephone starts to ring.

LUCY *and* ANGELA *jump, then quickly realise it's not* LUCY*'s mobile.*

COLLEEN: I'll get that.

She walks over to the phone and picks it up. Meanwhile, ANGELA *is a nervous wreck.*

ANGELA: Do you know what? I think I *will* have a glass of champagne.

MEG: [*surprised*] Are you sure, Ange?

ANGELA: Yeah, it's a special occasion.

She pours herself a glass of champagne, her hand shaking a little. Meanwhile...

COLLEEN: [*into phone*] Hello? Oh, hello Bill. [*Mouthing to* MEG] It's Dad.
LUCY: How about a medium super supreme?
ANGELA: But no anchovies.

> LUCY *rolls her eyes disparagingly re: the anchovies, as* COLLEEN *gasps into the phone.*

COLLEEN: [*into phone*] They did *what?!* Well that's just marvellous! [*Hand over receiver, to the girls*] They delivered the bridal registry gifts to Pakenham Upper!
MEG: What?!
COLLEEN: Did you fix it? Now are you sure it's sorted out? All right...

> COLLEEN *gestures to* MEG: *It's all right. Relieved,* MEG *turns her attention to a pizza menu. With* ANGELA *and* LUCY *she makes the pizza decision: Super Supreme, half with anchovies, half without. And garlic bread. Meanwhile...*

Bye then... Oh—Oh, Bill—you'll have to be here by eight thirty in the morning to pick up the place cards and ribbon—and I want Linda to tie the bows because you can't tie a bow to save yourself. Oh, and my spare pair of pantyhose are on top of the dryer. Thanks, bye.

> COLLEEN *hangs up and turns to the young women, enjoying the latest drama.*

Well what a shemozzle!
MEG: What happened? Is it fixed?
COLLEEN: It's all right. Your father's sorted it out. But apparently there are two James Davises getting married tomorrow, and one of them lives in Pakenham Upper.

> ANGELA *gives* LUCY *an excited look. Vindication.*

ANGELA: Two James Davises?
COLLEEN: Yes, apparently.
ANGELA: [*for* LUCY*'s benefit*] *Two* men called James Davis are getting married tomorrow?
COLLEEN: [*nodding*] That's what Bill said.
LUCY: Two separate weddings with two James Davises?
COLLEEN: [*getting impatient*] *Yes!*
LUCY: [*blurting to* ANGELA*, pleased*] Well that changes everything.
ANGELA: [*warning*] Lucy—

MEG: [*interrupting*] What do you mean, that changes everything?
LUCY: I don't know what I mean. [*Turning to* ANGELA] What do I mean?
ANGELA: I don't know.

Fade to black.

SCENE FOUR

Spotlight on ANGELA. *She stands in her bathrobe, toweling her hair dry as she talks directly to the audience.*

ANGELA: I like Lucy, I really do, but she makes me feel like I'm the kind of person who buys all their clothes at *Katies*. I've bought maybe two skirts and one top there in twenty years. And so what if I bought *everything* there? What would it matter? And why am I talking about *Katies*, anyway..? [*Sighs, composes herself*] Oh, I don't know... How can I explain a lifelong commitment to someone who doesn't want to understand? What could I say to her? That I look at John and I see my home? It sounds too cutesie for words, but it's true. I've always felt like that. Ever since we met. I was only seventeen, and he was my first ever boyfriend—well, except for Barry O'Brien, but that doesn't really count, because he only touched my breasts twice, and I cried afterwards. [*Gets a bit sidetracked*] I can't remember why I cried. Maybe I had my period? No, that's right, yeah—he pinched my nipples, and it really hurt. Anyway, I married the only guy I'd ever had sex with. Can you imagine what Lucy would think about that? Well, I *know* what she thinks. She thinks I'm a daggy mum from the suburbs who's had an easy ride. And she thinks I don't understand what's going on with James and Meg—but *she's wrong...*

[*Vulnerable*] The thing is, James is a nice man... And nice people make mistakes sometimes. He's probably torturing himself about it, and isn't that punishment enough? And he adores Meg. I can see it in his eyes. And as for her, well, I haven't seen her this happy since we won the Abba competition when we were in second class. Bjorn kissed her, and she got to hold Frida's hand, and she was so-o-o-o excited... Oh, except Mrs. Bacon took some photos and they didn't turn out. That was such a bummer. [*Stops, gets back to the point*] Anyway, the point is, Meg's ecstatic. And Lucy expects me to just just turn around and destroy that for her, without knowing any of the facts? I won't do it. [*A beat or two*] It's all very well for Lucy to be so self-righteous, but what's *she* got to lose? It's not *her* future she's playing with. And besides, friendship's not about gratifying your own ego, it's about doing what's best for your friend. And James is the best thing that's ever happened to Meg. I still believe that. And I know that men… and women, too… do things that they regret sometimes. But if the commitment's there, a couple can come out on the other side, with their relationship stronger and deeper than ever… [*Beat*] I don't want to be responsible for Meg missing out on that.

Fade to black.

SCENE FIVE

It's about two hours later.

Empty pizza boxes and garlic bread wrapping lie around, plus several empty and/or half-empty bottles of champagne.

COLLEEN *sits at the table, wearing a dressing gown. She's measuring out the silver ribbon and cutting it into appropriate lengths. She's concentrating madly, so she's not really listening to* LUCY *and* MEG.

LUCY *and* MEG *sit on* MEG*'s bed, wearing their pyjamas. They're both loosened up by alcohol.* MEG *is chirpy as she paints her toe nails, while* LUCY *reads* Who Weekly. LUCY *is more relaxed now that she knows there are two James Davises, but she still keeps glancing at a clock. It's about 9.50pm.*

MEG: Hey, I've got a good one, Luce—
LUCY: Okay, hit me with it.
MEG: If Brad Pitt and Johnny Depp were both in town on the same night, and they both wanted to see you, but you could only see one—which one would you see?
LUCY: [*grinning*] Define 'see'.

> MEG *grins back and gestures towards* COLLEEN, *who is concentrating on the ribbons: Don't get too graphic with Mum in the room.*

[*Laughing*] Johnny. Definitely.

MEG: [*surprised*] You wouldn't do it with Brad?
LUCY: [*shaking her head*] Nah. Johnny's much sexier.
MEG: [*dubiously*] You reckon?
LUCY: [*fervently*] God, yeah.
MEG: I don't know… That *Winona Forever* tattoo would put me off. Plus he's been sleeping with supermodels. I'd be too embarrassed when he saw all my wobbly bits.
LUCY: So do it in the dark.
MEG: Nah. I like Brad better anyway. He's *such* a spunk…
LUCY: Exactly. You really want to have sex with a guy who's physically perfect?
MEG: Yeah, I'm weird like that.

The women share a girlie chuckle, then…

Anyway, I can't do it with either of them. I'm an old married woman now, almost.

LUCY *is brought back to reality with a thud.*

LUCY: What's the time?
MEG: Ten to ten. Hey, Mum—
COLLEEN: Thirty-five, thirty-six, thirty-seven… Hmm?
MEG: If Paul Newman and… Michael Parkinson were both in town on the same night and—
COLLEEN: [*interrupting*] Thirty-nine!
MEG: What?
COLLEEN: There's only enough ribbon here for thirty-nine pews!
MEG: But you said you were going to get enough for forty!
COLLEEN: I did, Meg. I asked for forty metres. They must've measured it wrong—
LUCY: [*overlapping*] But you're not doing it in one metre lengths. You haven't got the tape measure, remember? So you don't know the exact length of the pieces.
COLLEEN: [*to* MEG] See? I *knew* I should've borrowed a tape measure! Now what are we going to do?
MEG: Well we'll just have to put bows on thirty-nine pews—
COLLEEN: We can't have an *uneven* number of bows!
MEG: Well then, we can put the bows on thirty-eight pews—
COLLEEN: [*overlapping*] No! I've worked it out in my head, Meg, and the bride's side will take up twenty pews!

LUCY: Well how many pews will James' side take up?
COLLEEN: About sixteen.
LUCY: Then you only need thirty-six ribbons, don't you?
COLLEEN: No. It's bad manners to have less ribbons on the groom's side.
LUCY: Then how about not having any ribbons?
COLLEEN: [*snapping sharply*] Don't be ridiculous!
MEG: Mum, Lucy's just trying to help. We'll just have to make do with thirty-nine ribbons—
COLLEEN: But it's an *uneven* number—
MEG: No-one will notice—
COLLEEN: Joyce Grainger will notice, I promise you.
LUCY: [*can't help herself*] Oh, for God's sake! Does this matter?!
MEG: Lucy… She didn't mean it, Mum.
COLLEEN: Oh, yes she did. I'm sorry if this wedding doesn't matter to *you*, Lucy, but it matters a lot to me, and a lot to Meg.
LUCY: I know. I'm sorry. I just don't think you should waste so much energy on ribbons. There must be more important things to worry about.

> *But the sub-text is lost on* MEG *and* COLLEEN.

COLLEEN: I just want Meg to have a nice day. Is that such a crime?

> MEG *moves over to her mother and puts her arm around her shoulders.*

MEG: Of course not, Mum. If you're still worried about the ribbon in the morning, we can get Dad to come a bit earlier and stop off at Myer on his way to the church. Or Linda could buy it—
COLLEEN: That's true. But how will she know what width to get?
MEG: She could come here and pick up the ribbons first. And they'll cut it for her at Myer.
COLLEEN: [*appeased*] Oh, all right, that makes sense.

> LUCY *takes another sip of her champagne, holding herself back, as the bathroom door opens and* ANGELA *emerges.*

ANGELA: I think I'm a bit drunk…

> *She flops down onto the bed like a rag doll.* MEG *and* COLLEEN *exchange worried looks.*

MEG: Are you okay?
ANGELA: Yeah... I'm fine...
COLLEEN: Are you sure, Angela?
ANGELA: [*quickly sitting up*] Yeah, I'm fine Mrs. Bacon.
COLLEEN: All right then. Well I'm off to bed. You should get to sleep soon too, Sweetheart.
MEG: I will, Mum. I just have to finish my toe nails.
COLLEEN: Angela, you're in with me, aren't you?
ANGELA: Yes Mrs. Bacon. I'll be in... sometime after ten thirty.

> LUCY *and* ANGELA *exchange a look as* COLLEEN *kisses* MEG *on the cheek.*

COLLEEN: Well, I'll see you on your special day...
MEG: 'Night, Mum... Sleep well...
LUCY/ANGELA: Goodnight Colleen/Mrs. Bacon [*etc*]

> COLLEEN *smiles warmly at* ANGELA *and tightly at* LUCY.

COLLEEN: Goodnight girls. Don't keep Meg up too late.
ANGELA: We won't.

> COLLEEN *exits.*

LUCY: Sorry about upsetting her, Meg—
MEG: Forget it, Luce. I've had fifteen years to get used to you two. [*Playfully pushing her off the bed*] Get off, go on...

> As LUCY *gets off the bed,* MEG *climbs back on and resumes painting her toe nails. In the meantime,* LUCY *assembles the folding bed.*

Hey, I've got another one: Ange—would you rather be a topless waitress or a parking officer?

> ANGELA *grimaces at the horrific options.*

ANGELA: Oh, yuk... They're both horrible... Can you lie about what you do for a living?
MEG: No, you have to go to parties and tell the whole truth.
LUCY: Shit. I'd be a topless waitress.

> *Lucy's mobile phone rings.*

Ohh! That's my mobile again—

> LUCY *and* ANGELA *exchange a look as* LUCY *grabs her phone:*

The moment of truth.

MEG: At ten o'clock on a Friday night? Why don't you turn it off?

LUCY: [*into phone*] Hello?

MEG: Who's going to ring someone at ten o'clock on a Friday?

    ANGELA *shrugs in what she hopes is a casual manner.*

LUCY: No, you've got the wrong number. Yeah, bye.

    She hangs up. She and ANGELA *exchange a look: The tension is killing them.*

MEG: Just turn it off, Luce—

ANGELA: [*frazzled*] Let's open another bottle!

    She flops down like a rag doll again.

    Fade to black.

SCENE SIX

Spotlight on COLLEEN. *She wears a floral nightie and carries a toiletries bag. Savouring a delicious feeling of anticipation, she addresses the audience directly.*

COLLEEN: You know, I opened a wedding account for Meg two weeks after she was born. It's added up to quite a nice amount now, much more than I'd ever thought, but then, we weren't expecting to wait thirty-three years... Oh, it did look like she was going to marry Paul when she was in her late twenties, but he got cold feet. It broke her heart I think, and she didn't meet James 'til quite a while later. And in the meantime the questions from our friends started. *So your* MEG*'s still single then?* And I'd smile and say *Oh, she's way too fussy.* But I could see they were feeling sorry for me and wondering where me and Bill had gone wrong. Honestly, it was so silly. And then they all started having grandchildren, and do you think we ever heard the end of *that?* I swear, if I'd had to look at one more baby photo... [*Allows herself a smug smile*] But anyway, it's all worked out for the best now, because Meg's got James—and he's a lawyer. And he owns a house *and* a flat—oh, not that that matters of course, but I have to say he's a lot more successful than any of Joyce Grainger's sons-in-law. [*Ponders that for a pleasing moment*] I've spent months planning every detail for tomorrow—because every girl deserves a beautiful wedding. She should be able to show off those photos forever and say 'That was the happiest day of my life and everything was perfect'. [*Suddenly tight*] Goodness knows you don't want people saying 'Is that a coffin in the corner?' like they say when they look at *my* wedding photos. But yes, there's a coffin behind me and Bill when we're signing the register. It looks like I'm balancing it on my left shoulder. 'Part bride, part pallbearer' some wag once said, and they thought it was funny, but it wasn't. [*The façade crumbles further*] It was supposed to be *my special day,* but there were grieving relatives crying on the front steps so we had to have our photos taken 'round the back of the church. We didn't want to upset them with our happiness—not that I was happy—because nothing was the way *I* wanted it—and I'm not just talking about the funeral—*I* didn't have *any* say in *anything*—But anyway, that was a long time ago, and it's Meg's turn now. And her wedding's going to be perfect—

[*Losing it again*] Because my mother—God rest her soul, is gone—so she can't hijack Meg's wedding like she did mine!

Fade to black.

SCENE SEVEN

It's about 10.15 now. More alcohol has been consumed. LUCY, ANGELA *and* MEG *are lazing around in their PJ's, indulging in some fun 'girl talk'. As* LUCY *tells an anecdote,* ANGELA *and* MEG *listen intently.* ANGELA *is a little tipsier than the other two.*

LUCY: ... Anyway, he was ringing her almost every day and asking her out to the movies and stuff, so finally Sue had to say to him, 'look—I like you, but I don't think I like you, you know...
MEG/ANGELA: [*Overlap, in unison*] Like *that.*
LUCY: Yeah. 'Cause she was trying to be fair—
MEG: [*nodding*] Like you do—
LUCY: Yeah. And *he* said 'Well I *was* hoping for more, but I really appreciate your honesty. And if friendship's all you can offer, I'd love to be your friend'.
ANGELA: Well, that's really nice, isn't it—?
LUCY: [*overlapping*] Yeah it was, but then two days later—are you

listening—*forty-eight hours later*—Sue thought 'well, friendship's a two way street, I guess *I* should call *him*'—so she rings him—and he tells her that he's really sorry to hurt her, but he just can't give her what she wants.

>ANGELA *and* MEG *laugh, gasp and shake their heads in a* Typical Man *gesture.*

ANGELA: Why did he do that?
LUCY: Who the hell knows?
ANGELA: And what did he think she wanted anyway?
LUCY: [*grinning*] To marry him of course.
ANGELA: But she was the one who said she didn't— [feel that way.]
LUCY: [*overlapping*] I know! But he's a man so that's not what he heard.
ANGELA: They're amazing, aren't they?
LUCY: [*nodding*] Awe-inspiring.

>*Silence for a moment, then...*

MEG: Imagine if you could harness the energy of the male ego and use it for good instead of evil? [*Beat*] Pass me the champers, Luce...
ANGELA: More for me too.
MEG: Are you sure, Ange?
ANGELA: [*overlapping, slightly sozzled*] You know what *I* don't get about men? Why so many of them want to be with women who, well... you know... aren't quite as intelligent as—
LUCY: [*overlapping*] Women who are *dumb*, Angela. Tell it like it is. A lot of guys want to be with dumb chicks.
MEG: Can you imagine anything more boring than having some dumb but good-looking guy at home, who cooked your meals and kept the house tidy and agreed with everything you said?

>*They stop and think about this for a moment...*

Actually, that sounds quite appealing...
LUCY: I could handle it for a while.
ANGELA: I don't know. I don't think I could have sex with a dumb guy...
LUCY: I could. I can. I have.
ANGELA: Really? How many?
LUCY: Times, or dumb guys?
ANGELA: Dumb guys.
LUCY: Just the one. A guy called Ben.

MEG: [*clearing her throat*] Hhhhm... Craig.
LUCY: Just the two.
ANGELA: And was it good?
LUCY: It was great until he opened his mouth. To *talk*.

    LUCY *and* MEG *laugh together.*

ANGELA: See? You *couldn't* be with a dumb guy. And we should be fair to men I suppose—
MEG: [*overlapping, jokingly*] Oh, why should we? That's no fun.
ANGELA: I mean, there are lots of men out there who don't want to be with dumb women either. Every brainy married woman has to be married to someone.
LUCY: Yeah, but hear that pivotal word 'married'? All the good men are taken.
MEG: Not necessarily. What about David?
LUCY: Yeah. Well. We'll see.
ANGELA: Who's David?
MEG: Lucy had a hot date last night.
ANGELA: Really?! Was it good? Is he nice?
LUCY: He's gorgeous, but he's *just* broken up with his girlfriend.
ANGELA: Well, Meg always says that's the best time to get them.
LUCY: [*grinning*] Yes, I'm familiar with that theory—
MEG: [*overlapping*] It's true. The good ones are only single for a week at a time, and you have to give them a few days to grieve, so that leaves you with a three day window of opportunity, and that's when you have to pounce.
ANGELA: This guy sounds perfect, then.
LUCY: Yeah, but I think he's still hung-up on Sandra.
MEG: No he's not. [*Turning to* ANGELA] He told Lucy he's over her. Those were his exact words: I'm over her.
ANGELA: But did he say 'I'm *over* her' or 'I'm over *her*'?
LUCY: See this is the thing. I couldn't tell.

    They all silently ponder this for a beat or two, then...

Look, it's *my* fault I can't find the right guy. I shouldn't have stuffed around so much in my twenties... It's like there's this amazing rock concert on, but instead of queueing early I got distracted, and by the time I got to the top of the line there were only seats with partial viewing left.

> LUCY *is amused by her own analogy, as are* MEG *and* ANGELA.

MEG: Oh thank you God… I don't want to rub it in, Luce, but this just makes me want to run right over to James' place and marry him *tonight*. God, I'm so glad I'll never have to go on another date.

> *This brings* ANGELA *and* LUCY *back to reality a bit. They exchange a worried look.*

LUCY: What's the time?

MEG: Twenty past ten. Oops. I've got to cleanse and tone.

> MEG *gets to her feet as Lucy's mobile starts ringing again.*

LUCY/ANGELA: [*startled*] Aaagh!

MEG: [*laughing*] Look at you two—nerves of steel. I thought you were going to turn that thing off…

> *As* LUCY *walks over to pick up her phone,* MEG *heads for the bathroom.*

I've never met anyone who gets so many phone calls on a Friday night. No-one ever rings me on a Friday…

LUCY: [*into phone*] Hello? Oh, hi Carol.

MEG: Carol? From work..?

> LUCY *nods 'casually' in response to* MEG'*s question.* MEG *waves, mouths the words:* Say hi from me.

LUCY: Oh, I'm just sitting here with Meg… and Angela… yeah… great, no, we had a pizza…

> MEG *exits into the bathroom, closing the door behind her.*

LUCY: [*lowering her voice*] Okay—She's in the bathroom. Yeah… yeah? Davis. [*Turning to* ANGELA] It's James Davis!

ANGELA: But there are *two*!

LUCY: [*snapping at her*] I know that! [*Into phone*] Does he live at Pakenham Upper? Well ask your friend to ask her. Shit!

ANGELA: What? What?

> ANGELA'*s tapping* LUCY *on the shoulder to get her attention.* LUCY'*s incredibly irritated. She slaps* ANGELA'*s hand away as she continues with the phone call.*

LUCY: Is she coming back? Well call me if she does. Thanks Carol. Bye. [*She hangs up, and turns to* ANGELA] Davis. That's all she knows. We'll have to ring the guy in Pakenham Upper—What's that number

where they connect you direct?
ANGELA: One-two-four-five-six—
LUCY: [*starting to press the numbers*] one-two-four-five—
ANGELA: [*interrupting*] But it's really expensive.
LUCY: I don't care! [*Into phone*] Oh hi—yes, James Davis, in Pakenham Upper— [*Crossing her fingers*] Thanks—Yes! They're connecting me—
ANGELA: What are you going to say?
LUCY: Fucked if I know. It's ringing! Oh, it's a machine—He sounds really old—hold on— [*She listens*] Shit, oh…God…

She looks like she doesn't know whether to laugh or cry.

ANGELA: What?!
LUCY: [*hanging up*] He's President of the Pakenham Seniors Club.
ANGELA: [*doesn't know whether to laugh or cry either*] Oh…

They look at each other in silence for a moment, the full implications dawning, then…

LUCY: Well, Naomi wouldn't be fucking a grandad. When Meg comes out of the bathroom we'll just have to tell her.
ANGELA: No! I still say we don't.
LUCY: Oh, what?! But it's *him!*
ANGELA: Yeah, but don't forget Carol said it's over now—
LUCY: So? What's that got to do with— [anything?!]
ANGELA: [*interrupting*] And he's made Meg happy. You can't deny that.
LUCY: Yeah, but only because she doesn't— [know about this.]
ANGELA: [*interrupting*] And *you* thought he was good for her too. You *told me* that—!
LUCY: Yeah, but I didn't know what he was doing—
ANGELA: But he's still the same person you liked, Lucy.
LUCY: Bullshit!
ANGELA: I don't think we should tell her.

LUCY looks at her like she's a complete moron.

LUCY: *What* is your problem?
ANGELA: [*firmly*] It's a bad idea.
LUCY: How can you *say* that?

ANGELA looks LUCY square in the eye. When she speaks again her tone is even firmer.

ANGELA: Look, I know Meg. You'll just have to trust me.

LUCY *would like to hit her over the head with a cricket bat, but instead she tries to reason with her.*

LUCY: Angela, it's nice that you don't want to hurt her, and if I thought that Meg and James could have what you and... [*Searching for* ANGELA*'s husband's name*] you and...

ANGELA: [*tersely*] John.

LUCY: You and John have, I wouldn't want to either. But there aren't many relationships as perfect as yours—

ANGELA: [*overlapping, irritated*] Ours isn't perfect—

LUCY: Okay, not perfect, but it's obviously been pretty smooth sailing compared to other people's—

ANGELA: Not always. We've had our ups and downs—

LUCY: Well yeah, but something like this would never be an issue with you guys—

ANGELA: [*hissing*] For God's sake, Lucy *I've* had an affair!

LUCY: *What?!*

ANGELA: [*eyes darting towards the bathroom*] I've had an affair.

LUCY: [*stunned*] *You've* had an affair?

ANGELA: [*nodding, low*] It was last year, and I didn't think I'd ever—

LUCY: [*interrupting*] Was he a friend of John's?

ANGELA: What? No! No way, as if I'd—look, I went to a teacher's conference and I met this man and I just, I never expected to do anything like that, but I'd only ever been with John and... it happened.

LUCY: *You've* had an affair?

ANGELA: Yes. Maybe I'm not quite as boring as you thought.

LUCY: I never said you were boring—

ANGELA: [*overlapping*] Anyway—it went on for a couple of months, but all it did was make me realise how lucky I am to have John, and I felt incredibly guilty, so I told him...

LUCY: You told him?

ANGELA *nods.*

Well there you go—

ANGELA: [*shaking her head*] If I had my time again, I wouldn't tell him—well, first of all I wouldn't *do it*—but if I did, I wouldn't tell him. It was horrible Lucy. I nearly lost him. We're only just back on track now. And if I hadn't told him, we wouldn't have gone through any of it.

    LUCY *is still stunned by this information.*

LUCY: And did Meg know about this?
ANGELA: Yes.
LUCY: Well, what did she say—?
ANGELA: [*overlapping, significantly*] She told me not to tell him.

    This hangs in the air for a moment. But LUCY*'s compulsive honesty propels her forward.*

LUCY: Yeah, all right—but everyone knows it's different when it's *you*. I still think she'd want to know.
ANGELA: I'm not sure she would.
LUCY: But what if she found out in six months and knew that we knew and didn't tell her? How would we feel then?
ANGELA: And if we *do* tell her, she might call off her wedding and miss out on fifty fantastic years with James. For all we know he'll never do it again.
LUCY: But I can't live with myself if I don't tell her the truth.
ANGELA: But maybe *she* couldn't live with herself if you did.

    The bathroom door opens and MEG *re-emerges, rubbing moisturiser into her face.*

MEG: What did Carol want?

    ANGELA *jumps in quickly before* LUCY *can answer.*

ANGELA: She's going to work tomorrow. She needs one of Lucy's files.
MEG: Oh…

    MEG *plonks herself onto the bed.* ANGELA *and* LUCY *look awkward—what should they do?*

[*Lightly*] It was probably really dumb to ex-foliate tonight. I'm going to have bulbous pimples popping up while I'm walking down the aisle.
ANGELA: No you won't.
MEG: [*grinning*] What are you standing there like idiots for? Sit down.

    She pats the bed beside her, but LUCY *and* ANGELA *sit at the table in a single, swift, self-conscious movement.* MEG *gives them*

> *an odd look, then starts playing with an empty champagne bottle, spinning it absent-mindedly...*

Hey, you know how they reckon wine's good for you now, for your heart and stuff—?

LUCY: Well, *red* wine is.

MEG: Oh, is it only *red* wine?

LUCY: Yeah.

MEG: Bummer. I was going to say 'do you reckon it's the same for champagne?'

LUCY: Not ten dollar bottles, Meg.

MEG: Shame...We would've all been brimming with good health after tonight...

> MEG *suddenly looks down at the bottle she's been absent-mindedly spinning...*

Hey, let's play *Truth or Dare!*

ANGELA: What?

MEG: Come on, it'll be fun! We'll spin the bottle. Who wants to go first?

LUCY: Truth or Dare?

MEG: Yeah. Come on—

> *A barely perceptible look between* LUCY *and* ANGELA: *This could be a way to work out whether* MEG *would want to know about James. A silent agreement.*

ANGELA: Okay. Let's do it.

LUCY: [*overlapping*] Yeah, okay, let's.

MEG: [*grinning*] Great.

> *They move over to join her on the bed as* MEG *grabs the bottle, preparing to spin...*

ANGELA: I haven't played *Truth or Dare* since I was sixteen. [*Reminding* MEG] You were there, remember? At Sally's place. I had to kiss—

> MEG *joins in. They say it in unison—*

ANGELA/MEG: Errr—Robert McDougall..!

MEG: Uggghh... with the green teeth. Gross. And he stuck his tongue in and twirled it around, remember—?

ANGELA: Errggh... stop it... I've spent seventeen years trying to forget.

MEG: [*laughing*] I'll go first—
LUCY: Go for it, Meg.

> MEG *spins the bottle and it lands on* ANGELA.

MEG: Ha! Ange!
ANGELA: Oh, no…
LUCY: Make it a juicy one.
MEG: Okay, truth or dare?
ANGELA: [*grimacing*] Truth.
MEG: Okay, let's see… [*Taking a few beats to think of a question*] Oh, I know—If John wanted to wear your lingerie, would you let him?
ANGELA: Depends. Do *I* want to wear it that day?

> MEG *and* LUCY *laugh in surprise at her blasé answer.*

MEG: Ange!
LUCY: You'd let him?
ANGELA: Anything except my Calvin Klein camisole. It's cream, and that's not a good colour for his complexion. My turn—

> *She starts spinning the bottle. The others are staring at her. She catches the look.*

ANGELA: [*laughing*] *I'm* allowed to crack jokes too.

> The bottle stops pointing to LUCY.

Lucy! Okay, truth or dare—
LUCY: [*subtext*] You know me. Truth every time.
ANGELA: All right, all right—Okay, let me think—okay—where's the strangest place you've ever had sex?
LUCY: At the City Baths. While people were doing laps all around us.
ANGELA: [*gasping*] You didn't?!
LUCY: I did. In the medium lane.
MEG: With Michael?
LUCY: Yeah.
MEG: [*laughing*] That'd be right.
ANGELA: [*impressed*] You could've been arrested, Lucy.
LUCY: Yeah, but we weren't. My turn.

> *She grabs the bottle and blatantly moves it so it's pointing towards* MEG.

Meg. You.

MEG: That was rigged! You didn't spin it!
LUCY: [*lying brazenly*]Yes I did. Truth or dare?
MEG: [*to* ANGELA] Did you see that? She rigged it.
LUCY: Come on—truth or dare?
MEG: Truth.

> *A barely perceptible look passes between* LUCY *and* ANGELA.

LUCY: Okay—Truth: If James was having an affair—right now, with twelve hours to go 'til the wedding, would you want to know?

> *Silence hangs in the air for a moment.* ANGELA *can hardly bear to look at* MEG. *They're both desperate to hear her answer.*

MEG: [*after a beat*] Dare.
LUCY/ANGELA: What?
MEG: I'll take the dare.
LUCY: Don't you want to answer the question?
MEG: I'll take the dare.
LUCY: You could take the dare and answer the question.
MEG: That's not the game, Luce.
ANGELA: God knows what dare she'll give you though Meg. If I was you I'd stick with the truth.
MEG: I said I'm taking the dare, okay?
LUCY: You're sure you don't want to take the truth?
MEG: Why? Can't you think of a good dare?
LUCY: [*thwarted*] Of course I can. All right… I dare you to ring room service and ask for a penis butter sandwich.

> MEG *and* ANGELA *guffaw etc.*

MEG: Oh, what?!
LUCY: You heard me. Ask them to send up a penis butter sandwich.
MEG: [*laughing*] I can't do that.
LUCY: Then answer the question.
MEG: No, I mean, I *can* do it, but it's so childish!
LUCY: Oh, derrr… I thought that was the whole point.
MEG: Here. Give me the phone— [*Grabbing the hotel phone, and looking at the numbers*] This is *so* embarrassing. What number's Room Service?
ANGELA: It's not too late to pick the truth.
MEG: It's okay. I'll do the stupid dare.

In spite of themselves, ANGELA *and* LUCY *can't help giggling as* MEG *dials the number.*

LUCY: They're going to know what room this is, you know. As soon as they pick it up—

ANGELA: [*overlapping*] Yeah, the number lights up—

MEG: [*overlapping*] Sssssh! [*Embarrassed, giggling etc*] Oh, hello. Umm… it's *Lucy Dean* from Room 304 here…

LUCY: [*calling into phone*] No, it's Meg Bacon!

MEG: [*pushing her away*] Umm… we were wondering if we could get some… umm… room service… Yeah, we'd like a round of, ah… of, umm… of… penis butter sandwiches—

ANGELA *and* LUCY *fall about laughing.*

[*Giggling*] Yeah, that's right… penis butter… Oh, you don't have that—?

LUCY: Then ask if they've got some vaginamite!

MEG *bursts into guffaws of laughter and hangs up the phone. They're all in fits of giggles.*

MEG: Vaginamite?!

ANGELA: What did they say—?

MEG: [*laughing*] He was so polite, the poor thing—

LUCY: Did he laugh?

MEG: No! I've never felt like such a dickhead. I'm going to get you for this—

MEG *takes the bottle and blatantly moves it so it's pointing at* LUCY.

MEG: Truth or Dare?

LUCY: [*another look to* ANGELA] Truth.

MEG: I want you to take the dare.

LUCY: No. I'm taking the truth.

MEG: Take the dare, you scumbag.

LUCY: No. Unlike *some people,* I'm not afraid of the truth.

ANGELA: It's Meg's right not to pick the truth, Lucy.

But the sub-text of the argument is lost on MEG, *who is busy thinking of a question.*

MEG: God, I can't think of a single question that would embarrass *you*…

ANGELA: I've got one.
LUCY: Okay. What is it?
ANGELA: Truth: Have you ever had sex with a woman?
LUCY: [*grinning*] Define sex.
MEG: [*laughingly shocked*] Lucy!
ANGELA: [*embarrassed*] Well, sex… you know. Penetration.
LUCY: Then no.
MEG: [*to* ANGELA] She would've told me if she'd—
LUCY: [*interrupting*] I've pashed one, though.

    MEG *and* ANGELA *look surprised and pretty impressed.*

MEG: You have not.
LUCY: I have so.
ANGELA: You've pashed a woman?

    LUCY *nods, enjoying the shock she's causing.*

MEG: Who?
LUCY: [*the slightest hint of discomfort*] Just someone.
MEG: What do you mean, just *someone?*
LUCY: Just a woman.
ANGELA: What? Tongues and everything?
LUCY: Yeah. I even touched her tits.
MEG: You did not!
LUCY: I did so.
ANGELA: What? *Under* her top?
LUCY: No, on the outside.

    MEG *is starting to look a little miffed.*

MEG: When did this happen?
LUCY: At that party at Doug's. After you went home.
MEG: That party at Doug's place? Last year?
LUCY: [*nodding, slightly awkward*] Yeah.
ANGELA: And what was it like?
LUCY: It was okay, but bristle's better.
MEG: I can't believe you didn't tell me. Why didn't you tell me?
LUCY: [*shrugging*] I don't know. Why? You're not upset?
MEG: Well, it's just a bit weird that something like this happened months ago and I didn't even know about it.
LUCY: But it was such a non-event, I didn't think to—

MEG: [*interrupting*] A what—? Lucy, you *pashed* a *woman*. That's an event.
LUCY: I'm sorry Meg, I didn't realise— [you'd feel this way.]
MEG: [*interrupting*] And I thought we told each other everything.
LUCY: [*itching to blurt it out*] It's not that I lied to you. I just didn't tell you.
MEG: *You're* the one who always says that deliberately not telling something is the same as lying.

> The door opens and COLLEEN *re-enters in her nightie. Her tone is scolding, as though she's talking to ten year old kids.*

COLLEEN: What's going on in here? You girls should be well and truly in bed by now.
MEG: Oh, sorry Mum. Did we wake you up? We're playing Truth or Dare.
COLLEEN: Truth or—don't be silly, Margaret. Come on, quickly, into bed. Do you want to look exhausted tomorrow?
MEG: Hardly. [*Pushing the other two off, climbs under the blankets*] Get off you two. All right, Mum. I'm in bed.

> LUCY *jumps onto the folding bed.*

LUCY: So am I. 'Night Colleen… [*Pointedly*] 'Night Angela.

> ANGELA *looks between them, worried that Lucy will spill the beans.*

ANGELA: I think I'll sleep out here with you two.
COLLEEN: Don't be silly. There's a free bed in the next room.
ANGELA: [*jumping in beside* MEG] Yeah, but there's plenty of room in here with Meg—
MEG: I'm a kicker, Ange. You'd have bruises under your bridesmaid's dress.
ANGELA: I don't mind.

> But COLLEEN*'s already pulling back the bedclothes. She practically drags* ANGELA *out of the bed.*

COLLEEN: [*scolding*] Don't be silly, Angela. You'll see the girls in the morning.
LUCY: [*pointedly*] Yeah. We'll see you in the morning.
ANGELA: [*thwarted*] All right then…

MEG: 'Night Ange. Sleep well.
ANGELA: 'Night, Meg. 'Night Lucy— [*Throwing a final warning look at* LUCY, *a joke laced with sub-text*] Don't do anything I wouldn't do.

And with that she turns, and mustering all the drunken dignity she can, opens the door and exits—straight into the wardrobe. She emerges, embarrassed, and scuttles off to the second bedroom.

Meanwhile COLLEEN *has turned off the main light and is about to follow...*

COLLEEN: 'Night then—
MEG: Mum, will you tuck me in?
COLLEEN: [*melting*] Oh, of course I will...

She walks over to MEG's *bed and tucks her in with maternal tenderness. She tucks her in, then she kisses her on the forehead.*

There you are. Snug as a bug in a rug. Now sleep tight 'til morning bright. Your very last night as a single girl...
MEG: Yeah...

As COLLEEN *walks past* LUCY, *there's an awkward moment where she's not sure whether she should tuck her in or not. She pauses, does a little two-step.*

LUCY: I'm all tucked. Thanks Colleen.
COLLEEN: [*relieved*] All right, well, goodnight then.
LUCY: 'Night.
MEG: 'Night Mum. Sleep well...

COLLEEN *exits.*

MEG *pops her head up above the bedclothes and grins across at* LUCY.

Can you turn the light off, Luce? I'm trapped here.
Her head pops down again.
LUCY: [*grinning*] Sure...

She sits up to turn off the lamp between the beds, but she doesn't flick the switch.

Listen, I'm sorry I didn't tell you about kissing that girl...

MEG: It's okay... I was just surprised... I didn't think we kept anything from each other...
LUCY: I didn't *deliberately* keep it from you.
MEG: [*mildly*] Oh, come on, Luce... You stuck your tongue down a woman's throat. It's not like you would've forgotten.
LUCY: Yeah, all right. I suppose I was embarrassed.
MEG: Why? With *me*? *I* wouldn't care.
LUCY: Yeah. I know, but I guess I just—
MEG: [*overlapping*] Look, anyway, I don't want to make a big deal of it, but I was surprised 'cause I've always loved how you don't censor yourself—
LUCY: [*interjecting*] Yeah, but—
MEG: [*over her*] You know me, I'm always watching what I say—not with you, but with everyone else—'cause I don't want to hurt their feelings or I'm worried about what they'll think, but you just come straight out with it. You're not scared to say things that people don't want to hear. That's one of the things I love about you.
LUCY: [*this is torture*] Thanks.
MEG: Anyway, you're officially forgiven. Can you turn off the light? If I don't get eight hours my eyes will be bloodshot.
LUCY: Sure.

> LUCY *turns off the light and lies down.*

MEG: Goodnight, you big lezzo.
LUCY: 'Night.

> *They both lie still in their beds. Silence for several beats, then* LUCY *suddenly sits bolt upright in bed and turns the light back on.*

　Meg...
MEG: [*eyes closed*] Mmm...?
LUCY: James has been having an affair.

> *Fade to black.*
>
> *End of Act One.*

ACT TWO

SCENE EIGHT

It's the next morning. About 7.15am.

The hotel room is empty save a hung-over ANGELA, *who is freshly showered and wears her bridesmaid's dress. She drops a Berocca into a glass of water as she talks on the phone.*

ANGELA: [*into phone*]Yeah, he's been sleeping with Naomi Bartlett! She's invited to the wedding, and everything! No, she threw Lucy out at about midnight. No, her mum doesn't know anything, and Meg doesn't know I know… [*Looking around, winces as the movement hurts her head*] I'm not sure. They weren't here when I got up… but I thought I should get dressed in case… But I just wanted to ring and…tell you I love you and…

A key is heard in the door, and COLLEEN*'s voice.*

COLLEEN: [*off*] Oh, I've just thought—!
ANGELA: [*into phone, hastily*] Got to go! Bye!

    ANGELA *slams the phone down as the door opens and* MEG *and* COLLEEN *enter. They're both extremely agitated, especially* MEG. COLLEEN *is wearing her Mother of the Bride outfit.*

COLLEEN: [*to* MEG, *as they enter*] The seating at Table Eleven—!
MEG: [*over her, to* ANGELA, *curtly*] Has James rung?
ANGELA: No.
MEG: Shit.

    She stomps straight over to the phone.

COLLEEN: Oh Angela, you're dressed. You look lovely.
ANGELA: Thanks Mrs Bacon. So do you.

    Meanwhile MEG *punches some numbers aggressively into the phone.* COLLEEN *maintains her forced cheer. She's nervy, on edge.*

COLLEEN: We've just been downstairs giving Meg's father the name cards. Linda's going to get some extra ribbon—
ANGELA: Great. So it's all under control— [*then?*]

COLLEEN: [*overlapping, to* MEG] Anyway, as I was saying—this means we *can* invite your Great Uncle Reg—but how are we going to explain inviting him at the last minute?

MEG: [*agitated, into phone*] Be there... be there... be there...

COLLEEN: And we can't put him at Table Eleven—

MEG: [*overlapping*] Ssshh! Shit! [*Listening impatiently to James' outgoing message*] James it's me again for the fiftieth time. Why haven't you turned this thing back on yet? Can you call me at the hotel please? Bye. [*She hangs up*] Shit. Shit. Shit. [*To* COLLEEN, *re: the language*] Sorry.

COLLEEN: [*wincing*] It's all right.

ANGELA: Meg, are you okay?

MEG: [*overlapping, tersely*] No! But I don't want to talk about it.

COLLEEN: Neither do we, Sweetheart. Not if *you* don't. Now, I'm thinking we could move the Radners from Table Four to Table Eleven and put Great Uncle Reg and the vegetarian at Table Four—?

MEG: [*irritably*] Whatever—

ANGELA: Can I get anyone a cup of tea—?

COLLEEN: Do you think your cousin Mark would have left Ballarat yet?

MEG: How would I know?

COLLEEN: He could pick up Uncle Reg on the way—but why should some vegetarian we've never met be at Table Four—?

> But meanwhile MEG *has caught sight of herself in a silver lid from the room service breakfast. She lifts it up, stares into it in horror.*

MEG: Mum, I don't care! Shit, look at me. I look terrible.

ANGELA: No you don't.

COLLEEN: You look beautiful, Meg—

MEG: Oh, come on! I've got bags under my eyes and I'm white as a a ghost—

COLLEEN: [*more and more uptight*] You look lovely—!

MEG: [*overlapping, almost yelling*] I look disgusting—!

COLLEEN: All you need's a bit of makeup—

MEG: And how am I supposed to keep that on?! I can't stop crying! [*Blowing her nose loudly*] I'm going to look ugly walking up the aisle. And everyone will think 'She should be glowing, but she's all tired and haggard. What's happened?'

COLLEEN: Just a *little bit* of makeup—!
MEG: I don't need makeup! I need a fucking miracle!

> COLLEEN *cringes at the language as the phone rings.* MEG *leaps for it instantly.*

Thank God!

> *Their uptight energy is communicating itself to* ANGELA, *in spite of her best efforts. And the hang-over headache isn't helping.*

ANGELA: [*contained tension*] Mrs. Bacon? A cup of tea?
COLLEEN: [*distractedly*] Yes, all right.
MEG: [*into phone*] James?! Oh, hi Dad. Yeah, we're getting ready—
ANGELA: Earl Grey or English Breakfast?
MEG: [*snarling*] Nothing! I'm fine! Yeah, hang on a second— [*Holding the phone out to* COLLEEN, *angrily*] What did you say to him?!
COLLEEN: [*lying*] I didn't say anything!
MEG: It's something about the ribbons. And don't be on for long.

> COLLEEN *takes the phone from* MEG. MEG *stomps away and gets a packet of bandaids from her toiletries bag.*

ANGELA: Mrs Bacon? English Breakfast?
COLLEEN: [*ignoring her*] Yes Bill..? [*Lowering her voice*] Yes, she's still upset... No, I don't know— [why.]
MEG: [*overlapping, shut-up!*] Mum!

> ANGELA *has interpreted the 'yes' and 'no' as conflicting responses to her tea bag question. As* COLLEEN*'s conversation continues, she waves two tea bags in front of her face, hoping for a response that doesn't come.*

COLLEEN: [*into phone*] Anyway—the ribbons? No, I said I want Linda to tie them...What? But Myer doesn't open for another forty-five minutes—there's no point waiting out the front now—can you go and get her?
ANGELA: [*sighing*] I'll make you an English breakfast, then.
COLLEEN: [*into phone*] Now listen, I need you to ring Uncle Reg and invite him. But first ring Mark and ask if he can pick Uncle Reg up on his way through from Ballarat. And you'll need to go to the reception centre and move the place cards—put the Radners on Table Eleven and Uncle Reg and—ah— [*Turning to* MEG] What's the vegetarian's name?

MEG: [*snarling*] How should I know?!
COLLEEN: [*snarling back*] I'm only asking, Margaret! Hold on, Bill—
> *She hurries over, grumpily grabs the seating plan and goes back to the phone.* ANGELA *is really tense now too. She's boiling the kettle.*

ANGELA: You want a cup of tea, Meg?
MEG: [*overlapping, looking in the mirror*] Look at that. I've got broken capillaries all over my face—
ANGELA: No you haven't. You haven't got any.
MEG: Bullshit Ange. I'm covered in them.
COLLEEN: [*into phone*] His name's Paul Whelan—I don't know *who* the man is, Bill, let's not get into that—
MEG: [*waving the bandaids aggressively*] And to top it all off, I can't even *walk* in my bloody wedding shoes!
> *She's unwrapping large bandaids to put on her ankle.*

COLLEEN: [*into phone*] Anyway, put him on Table Four with Uncle Reg—no, I can't leave him on Table Eleven because that would mean separating the Graingers!
> ANGELA *takes a cup of tea over to* COLLEEN *and waits for her to finish her call.*

[*Into phone*] Yes, all right. Good. Right. We'll see you soon then. Bye.
> *She hangs up just in time to see* MEG *unwrapping the bandaids. She pushes past* ANGELA, *ignoring the cup of tea she's made for her.* ANGELA's *getting grumpy now.*

[*Snapping, shocked*] What are you doing?!
MEG: What does it look like I'm doing?! I'm putting a bandaid on my ankle!
COLLEEN: You can't put a bandaid on your ankle! People will see it when you do the bridal waltz!
MEG: But I won't be able to do the bridal waltz if I don't! My bloody shoes kill me!
COLLEEN: I told you to wear them around the house!
MEG: I did. That's when I got the blisters!
COLLEEN: Well for heaven's sake, Margaret! Why didn't you buy transparent bandaids?!

MEG: There's no such thing!
COLLEEN: There is so! Angela, can't you buy transparent bandaids?!

> ANGELA *can't contain herself any longer. She's thoroughly drawn into the argument.*

ANGELA: Those ones are fine. They're flesh-coloured.
COLLEEN: They're not flesh-coloured! *Look* at them! They don't match her ankle!
ANGELA: [*grumpily*] I think they do!
COLLEEN: Oh, rubbish! They're a totally different shade of beige!
MEG: [*screaming*] Well I'm sorry if my ankle's the wrong colour, Mum! Why don't I just *paint* my ankle?!
ANGELA: [*muttering to herself*] Bloody Lucy! I *knew* this would happen!
COLLEEN: [*over* ANGELA, *trying to calm* MEG] Oh look, it'll be all right. We'll just have to make do with—

> *But* MEG *isn't listening. She can't believe what she's just heard.*

MEG: [*interrupting, to* ANGELA] What did you say?!

> ANGELA*'s expression says it all: Ooops, busted.*

What did you say just then?
ANGELA: Nothing. I was just saying it's a shame that you and Lucy—
MEG: [*overlapping*] You *knew* about it, didn't you—?! [*Turning on* COLLEEN] Did you know too?!
COLLEEN: Know what?
MEG/ANGELA: [*snapping in unison*] Nothing!

> *An awkward silence as* COLLEEN *looks from* MEG *to* ANGELA, *not sure what to do with herself.*

COLLEEN: I'm sure the bouquets should be here by now. I might just ring Reception and check. I'll just—I think I'll do that from *my* room.

> *And she hastily exits, leaving* MEG *staring at* ANGELA *in shock.*

MEG: I can't believe this…
ANGELA: I'm so sorry, Meg. I told Lucy not to tell you—
MEG: You *what?!*
ANGELA: If it was up to me, we wouldn't have told you. I know how you feel about it—
MEG: [*overlapping*] You wouldn't have *told me?!* How could you know something like this and not tell me?!

This stops ANGELA *in her tracks. She's totally flummoxed.*

ANGELA: But I thought you wouldn't want to— [know.]

MEG: [*overlapping*] I can't believe you were going to keep me in the dark. I thought you were my friend.

ANGELA: [*flummoxed*] But I am—

MEG: Huh. Some friend.

ANGELA: But... but... you threw Lucy out for telling you.

MEG: At least she showed me some respect. You were going to let me look like a fool on my wedding day.

ANGELA: I'm sorry Meg... I didn't see it that way...

MEG: Well that's how *I* see it.

ANGELA: But... You told me not to tell John...

MEG: So? That was John. This is James. This is *me,* Ange.

ANGELA: So you do want to know?

MEG: Yes. No. I don't know. Oh, what the hell would I know? I just... I don't like people knowing stuff about my life that *I* don't...

ANGELA: Of course not... I'm sorry, Meg. I thought I was doing the right thing...

MEG: Oh, I know you did, but... if there's ever anything else I should know, I want you to tell me, okay?

ANGELA: [*nodding*] Of course.

MEG: You'll tell me?

    ANGELA *reaches across and takes her hand.*

ANGELA: Of course I will.

    They smile at each other sadly as COLLEEN *re-enters somewhat tentatively.*

COLLEEN: Well, the bouquets aren't here yet, but I'm sure they're not far away... Why don't I help you with that bandaid Sweetheart?

MEG: Thanks Mum.

    COLLEEN *walks over to* MEG *with forced cheer, determined to keep things nice.*

COLLEEN: You know, now that I look at it, you can't even notice it.

    There's a knock at the door. ANGELA *looks at the door, still a bit dazed.*

ANGELA: I'll get that.

She starts walking towards the door.

COLLEEN: It'll be the bouquets.

MEG: [*overlapping*] Or it could be Naomi.

ANGELA *stops dead in her tracks. Did she really hear that?*

ANGELA: *What?*

MEG: Naomi's going to step in for Lucy.

ANGELA: *What..?*

COLLEEN: Oh, didn't we tell you? Naomi's taking Lucy's place.

ANGELA: *Naomi is..?*

MEG: Yeah.

ANGELA: Naomi *who..?*

MEG: Naomi Bartlett.

ANGELA: [*weakly*] Naomi Bartlett's going to be a bridesmaid..?

MEG: [*getting impatient*] Yes.

There is another knock at the door. ANGELA *still doesn't move.*

COLLEEN: For heaven's sake Angela, will you let her in?

ANGELA: Yeah… ah, right… of course…

ANGELA *walks to the door, unable to believe the awfulness of the situation. She's officially in hell as she opens the door to an attractive woman in her late twenties,* NAOMI.

NAOMI*'s forced smile is only just managing to hide her extreme nervousness.*

NAOMI: Hi!

ANGELA: [*icily*] Hi.

ANGELA*'s hostile greeting sends* NAOMI *into a panic that she has to try and hide.*

MEG: Naomi, hi! You've met Ange before, haven't you?

NAOMI: [*nervously smiling*] Yeah, hi Angela…

MEG: And this is my mum, Colleen…

COLLEEN *walks over and shakes* NAOMI*'s hand.*

COLLEEN: [*warmly*] Nice to meet you, Naomi.

NAOMI: Nice to meet you too, Mrs. Bacon.

COLLEEN: Oh, call me Colleen.

MEG: [*Re: herself and* COLLEEN] Will you excuse us for just one sec? We've got a bandaid situation—

NAOMI: Yeah, sure…

> COLLEEN *goes back to* MEG *and starts applying the bandaid. Meanwhile* NAOMI *does everything she can to avoid meeting* ANGELA*'s eyes. But* ANGELA *comes around to stand in front of her, giving her a completely unambiguous look:* I know what's going on. *While* MEG *and* COLLEEN *are occupied with the bandaid, the following conversation takes place between* ANGELA *and* NAOMI*; via gestures and lip-reading:* What the hell are you doing here?! I couldn't get out of it! I couldn't say no! Get out! I'd love to, but how can I?!

> MEG *and* COLLEEN *are oblivious to all this because they're talking bandaids:*

MEG: Mum, that's crooked!
COLLEEN: Well hold your foot still!
MEG: It *is* still!
COLLEEN: And it's *not* crooked, Meg—
MEG: It's on a forty-five degree angle! Look!
COLLEEN: All right, all right—

> *She pulls the bandaid off.*

MEG: Oww!
COLLEEN: Don't be silly, Margaret. That didn't hurt.

> *She re-applies the bandaid at a straight angle.*

   There you are. All right?
MEG: Yes. Thank you.
COLLEEN: All done.

> *They both turn their attention to* NAOMI. ANGELA *feels she has to do something.*

ANGELA: Meg—

> *But* MEG *walks straight past her to* NAOMI, *warm and welcoming.*

MEG: [*overlapping*] Thanks for getting here so quickly, Naomi—
NAOMI: Glad I could help.
MEG: [*kissing her*] You're a lifesaver—!
ANGELA: [*interrupting, tightly*] Meg, can I talk to you for a second? Alone?
MEG: [*distracted*] What..?

ANGELA: Can I talk to you for a second? In private?
MEG: What about—?
NAOMI: [*interrupting, desperately cheerful*] So, how are preparations going?!
COLLEEN: Not as quickly as they should be—
ANGELA: [*to* MEG] I just want to talk to you for one second—
COLLEEN: [*interrupting, briskly*] There's been far too much gossiping already, girls. Look at the time—!
MEG: [*looking at her watch*] Oh yeah, you're right Mum—
ANGELA: It'll only take a couple of seconds—
MEG: Not now, Ange.
ANGELA: [*overlapping*] But I really need to—
COLLEEN: Not *now,* Angela! We need to get Naomi dressed—
MEG: And *me.*
COLLEEN: And you, of course Sweetheart. As if we'd forget the bride..!
ANGELA: [*interrupting, desperately*] But—it's not going to fit!

    MEG *and* COLLEEN *stop and look at* ANGELA *in surprise.*

MEG: What?
ANGELA: The dress! She's shorter than Lucy. Aren't you Naomi?

    NAOMI*'s just as keen to get out of there as* ANGELA *is to have her leave.*

NAOMI: Yeah, I *am* a lot shorter—!
MEG: You're not *a lot* shorter—
ANGELA: The dress is going to be way too long.
NAOMI: Yeah, I wouldn't want to spoil the effect—
MEG: A couple of inches won't make any difference.
ANGELA: But mine's cocktail length. [*Turning to* COLLEEN] It'll look untidy.

    COLLEEN *visibly reacts to his horrific scenario.* NAOMI *seizes on it.*

NAOMI: I'd hate to make the wedding party look untidy. Maybe you should just have one bridesmaid—?
ANGELA: Yeah, I think it'd be better to just have one—!
COLLEEN: [*nearing the end of her tether*] We *can't* have *one* bridesmaid because that would mean only having *one* groomsman, and we can't get hold of James to tell him. And there's only a slight difference in

height anyway, so... [*Smiling maternally at all three*] I suggest that we all relax and enjoy Meg's special day together, because that's all that counts, isn't it..?

> MEG *smiles back. In spite of everything, she really wants to enjoy this morning.*

MEG: Yeah, you're right, Mum. I've been waiting thirty-three years for this, so let's just have some fun, eh?

> NAOMI *and* ANGELA *give strangled smiles in return.*

ANGELA/NAOMI: Yeah/Yeah, of course/Great [*etc*]
COLLEEN: Just slip off your shoes for us, will you Naomi..?

> *Meanwhile* ANGELA *gives it one more try.*

ANGELA: [*low*] Meg...

> *But* MEG *silences her with a warm hug.*

MEG: It's all right... Just don't do it to me again.

> ANGELA *smiles limply as* MEG *breaks the hug and starts heading to the wardrobe.*

Now let's get you into this dress, Naomi.
COLLEEN: [*following her*] But maybe we should try the shoes first.
MEG: Mum, can you relax about the shoes? Please? I think the dress is a bit more important.

> *As* COLLEEN *and* MEG *fuss over at the wardrobe,* ANGELA *gestures frantically for* NAOMI *to leave while they're not looking.* NAOMI *runs to the door, then remembers her handbag, running back to pick it up just as* MEG *looks over—*

Okay Naomi, get your gear off.

> *Thwarted,* NAOMI *starts taking off her skirt and top. Meanwhile* MEG *and* COLLEEN *are fussing with the bridesmaid's dress.*

COLLEEN: Slip it off the hanger carefully, Meg. We don't want to crumple it— [*Looking at the dress, then over at* NAOMI] Oh, I'm sure it'll fit...

> NAOMI *slips off her skirt and top to reveal beautiful french lingerie (the kind a woman buys when she's met a new man).*

MEG: Wooh... gorgeous undies. Who's the lucky guy?

NAOMI: [*smiling awkwardly*] What?! Oh, no-one.

> *She tries to grab the bridesmaid's dress, but* MEG *playfully holds it out of reach as she teases her for more information.*

MEG: [*playfully*] Come off it. You don't buy this kind of stuff for *yourself*. You would have had to mortgage your flat for this. Who is he, and how come I haven't heard about him?

NAOMI: [*grabbing the dress*] Oh, it was just a guy. And it's over, anyway.

ANGELA: [*dripping with sarcasm*] Oh, what a shame.

> NAOMI *slips the dress over her head, managing to disappear for a precious second. Meanwhile* MEG *and* COLLEEN *look a little surprised by* ANGELA*'s tone, but there are too many other things to worry about.*

COLLEEN: Well quickly, help her. Come on Meg—

> MEG *and* COLLEEN *help* NAOMI *slip the dress down over her.*

NAOMI: It feels like it should fit…

ANGELA: [*pointedly*] Does it really?

NAOMI: [*oops*] Well, no, ah, no, maybe not.

COLLEEN: Don't be silly. It's going to be fine!

MEG: Let's do up the zip before we say that, Mum… Ange..?

ANGELA: What? Oh, sure… I'll just…

> ANGELA *starts doing up the zip, 'accidentally' pinching* NAOMI*'s skin in the process.*

NAOMI: Ouch!

ANGELA: [*totally insincere*] Sorry.

> ANGELA *fastens the zip right up to the top. The dress looks to be quite a good fit.*

MEG: Oh, it's pretty good, thank God!

COLLEEN: What did I tell you? It looks fine.

ANGELA: I still think it's way too long.

NAOMI: Yeah, I think it might be too long too.

> COLLEEN *and* MEG *stand back and look at the dress length appraisingly.*

MEG: No way. It's lovely, isn't it Mum?

COLLEEN: It's fine. Turn around for us, Naomi—

NAOMI *does a quick turn around in a circle.* MEG *and* COLLEEN *like what they see.*

No, that length is fine...

MEG: It's lovely.

COLLEEN: And thank goodness for that! Now let's see if the shoes fit. Angela, can you get Lucy's shoes please?

ANGELA: [*sullenly*] Yes.

As ANGELA *stomps over to the wardrobe and grabs Lucy's shoes...*

MEG: [*to* NAOMI] Show us your feet—Oh, they look about right...

COLLEEN: Yes, the shoes should be fine...

ANGELA *makes a point of staring at* NAOMI*'s feet.*

ANGELA: You reckon? Her feet are much fatter than Lucy's.

She thrusts the shoes at NAOMI *with such force that she almost falls over backwards.*

[*Thrusting the shoes at her*] Here.

NAOMI: [*almost falling over*] Oh—!

COLLEEN: Careful, Angela.

ANGELA: Sorry, Naomi.

MEG *and* COLLEEN *look at* ANGELA *in bemusement, but don't comment. Meanwhile* COLLEEN *is taking* LUCY*'s shoes out of the box.*

COLLEEN: Well quickly, let's try them on—

She hands the shoes to NAOMI. *In spite of the awfulness of the situation, in true female fashion* NAOMI *finds herself captivated by the shoes.*

NAOMI: Oh wow... they're beautiful....

MEG: You like them?

NAOMI: Yeah, they're gorgeous... And I love the shine...

COLLEEN*'s lips instantly purse and* MEG *rolls her eyes in amusement.*

[*Puzzled*]What..?

MEG: Don't get Mum started on the shiny part. It's a tad controversial.

NAOMI: Oh... Well, here goes...

MEG: Good luck Cinderella...

COLLEEN: Quickly. Do they fit—?

> *They all watch anxiously as* NAOMI *slips her foot into the shoe. She wiggles it around.*

NAOMI: Yeah, they fit—

MEG: Phew.

COLLEEN: Thank Goodness for that—!

ANGELA: [*through gritted teeth*] They don't look like they fit.

NAOMI: [*oops again*] Well actually, maybe, yeah now that I—yeah, I think they're a fraction too big.

COLLEEN: Where are they too big? In the toes?

NAOMI: [*walking a few steps*] Yeah, mainly in the toes.

> COLLEEN *starts briskly heading for the bathroom.* ANGELA *follows, calling after her—*

ANGELA: Well, we can't have a bridesmaid with shoes that don't fit—

COLLEEN: [*overlapping*] Rubbish. We'll just use a bit of tissue—

> *She emerges from the bathroom with a roll of toilet paper.*

MEG: [*joking*] Mum's the improviser from hell.

> COLLEEN *plonks herself on the end of the bed and starts ripping up the toilet paper.* MEG *sits down beside her.*

COLLEEN: Here, give me the shoes, Naomi—

> NAOMI *gives her the shoes.* COLLEEN *passes one to* MEG, *then demonstrates.* MEG *follows her lead.*

Now, if we just… pull off the paper, then fold it like this… and put a little in the toe of the shoes… like so…

> *During all this,* NAOMI *and* ANGELA *are exchanging silent looks.* NAOMI'*s look says* I hate this as much as you do, but I can't get out of it now.

And that should fill up the gap— [*Handing the shoes back*] Here Naomi, try that.

> NAOMI *puts the shoes back on with difficulty, and walks a few stilted, slow steps. They're way too tight now, and they're causing her pain.*

NAOMI: [*trying to turn a painful grimace to a smile*] That's great, Mrs. Bacon. Yeah… They feel fine now...

COLLEEN: Oh, good.
MEG: You're a genius, Mum.
COLLEEN: Well, what a relief… The dress *and* the shoes!

> MEG *suddenly gets a little emotional as she looks at* NAOMI *and* ANGELA *in their matching bridesmaids' outfits. She nudges her mother.*

MEG: Oh, look…

> *They both gaze at* NAOMI *and* ANGELA, *moved.*

I just want to say… when Lucy got stomach cramps I didn't know what I was going to do… I'm so glad you said yes at such short notice… I know this is a big ask Naomi, and I really appreciate it.

> MEG *emotionally pulls* NAOMI *into a hug. Then she pulls* ANGELA *into the hug too.*

> ANGELA *can't resist another deeply sarcastic comment.*

ANGELA: Yeah. You're such a *good friend*, Naomi.

> COLLEEN *notes* ANGELA*'s sarcasm. She claps briskly to break up the hug.*

COLLEEN: Come on, girls! The clock's ticking!

> *As the hug breaks,* COLLEEN *excitedly turns to* MEG.

It's time for you to put on your dress, Sweetheart!
MEG: Okay. I'll go grab the old bag of rags…!
COLLEEN: [*laughing*] Oh, Meg..!

> *She starts walking into the next room.* NAOMI *stumbles after her painfully, desperate to get away from* ANGELA*'s icy gaze.*

NAOMI: Here—I'll help you!
MEG: Thanks Naomi.

> *As soon as* MEG *and* NAOMI *leave the room,* COLLEEN*'s smile vanishes. She brusquely pulls* ANGELA *aside.*

COLLEEN: [*hissing, low*] What in heaven's name are you doing?
ANGELA: What do you mean?
COLLEEN: Why are you being so horrible?
ANGELA: I'm not.
COLLEEN: Yes you are. You're being nasty to poor Naomi.

ANGELA: 'Poor' Naomi?
COLLEEN: Yes. Poor Naomi. She's doing Meg a big favour in case you hadn't noticed.
ANGELA: [*sarcastically*] Well isn't Meg lucky to have a friend like *her*?

> COLLEEN *is totally flummoxed by* ANGELA*'s out of character nastiness.*

COLLEEN: What's wrong? *Why* are you being so horrible?

> ANGELA *pauses for a beat, then makes a spontaneous decision.*

ANGELA: All right, Colleen…

> COLLEEN *reacts to her Christian name.*

I'll tell you why—

> *But* COLLEEN *instantly puts her hands over her ears.*

COLLEEN: [*hastily interrupting*] I don't want to know why, I just want you to stop it. It won't kill you to be pleasant for Meg's sake.

> MEG *and* NAOMI *return with the wedding dress in its plastic cover and* MEG*'s veil.* NAOMI *looks like she's not far from tears.*

MEG: [*excitedly*] Okay, here goes. Will you help me get into this thing?
COLLEEN: Of course, Sweetheart. Come on Angela!

> ANGELA *and* COLLEEN *unzip the wedding dress and remove it from its plastic as* MEG *starts getting undressed. Meanwhile* NAOMI *hovers, holding the veil.*

Now, be careful of the zip. We don't want to snag it—
ANGELA: Oh, it's beautiful fabric..!
COLLEEN: Yes, it's silk de-lustred satin.

> ANGELA *takes the plastic cover away and turns to see* MEG *in full bridal lingerie.*

ANGELA: [*trying to be pleasant for Meg's sake*] Woooh, gorgeous…
NAOMI: [*a nervous wreck*] Yeah, gorgeous…
MEG: Do you think James will approve?
NAOMI: I wouldn't know! [*Collecting herself*] I mean, yeah, of course, what man wouldn't?

> NAOMI *tries to smile casually, but her lip starts trembling. During the following, she starts crying in spite of all her best efforts.*

> ANGELA *quickly shoves her out of the way so* MEG *won't see her tears.* COLLEEN *is oblivious. She's totally focused on the wedding dress.*

COLLEEN: All right... if we just gently open it up like this... and put it down towards the ground... Angela, just pull that out for me will you?

ANGELA: This bit?

COLLEEN: No this bit. That's right. All right Meg, you step over the top...

> *In spite of the circumstances,* MEG *is clearly feeling the magic of the moment.*

MEG: Here goes...

COLLEEN: Gently now... That's right, slowly... Now pull it up very gently...

> ANGELA *and* COLLEEN *pull the beautiful, heavy, voluminous dress up higher.*

MEG: It's happening...! I'm starting to feel like a bride..!

COLLEEN: Put your arms through here, Meg, like that. No, both arms—

> ANGELA *gently touches the beading on the bodice.*

ANGELA: This beading's just beautiful.

MEG: You don't think it's too much?

COLLEEN: Don't be silly, Meg. It's exquisite...

> MEG *is now in the dress. She looks absolutely beautiful.*

[*Emotionally*] Oh, look at you...

MEG: Isn't it gorgeous..?

ANGELA: You look beautiful, Meg...

MEG: I feel like Cinderella going to the ball.

COLLEEN: [*emotionally*] You look absolutely beautiful...

> NAOMI *sniffles loudly.* ANGELA *shoves her out of the way again, unnoticed by* COLLEEN *and* MEG.

Well come on, Angela. Help me do her up.

> ANGELA *and* COLLEEN *start doing up the tiny pearl buttons on the back of* MEG's *dress, while* NAOMI *tries to keep a low profile, quietly crying her heart out.*

ANGELA: Oh, I love these little pearl buttons...
MEG: I wanted a zip but James wanted these. He's going to undo them with his teeth one at a time... Sorry Mum. Too many details?
COLLEEN: [*focused on the buttons*] Keep still.
MEG: Naomi, where are you hiding? What do you think?

> *She tries to pull away, but* ANGELA *pulls her back.*

ANGELA: She loves it.

> *Meanwhile* NAOMI *is looking for somewhere, anywhere to hide. But too late—*

MEG: I asked Naomi, Ange. [*Breaking free of* ANGELA*'s grasp*] What do you think?

> *Trapped,* NAOMI *tries to smile, but there's no mistaking the fact that she's crying.*

NAOMI: You look beautiful, Meg...
MEG: Oh, you're crying...

> NAOMI *tries to smile through her tears. She doesn't trust herself to speak.*

MEG: That's so sweet... [*Joking, to* COLLEEN *and* ANGELA] Why aren't you big slackers crying?

> *At that moment there is a knock at the door.*

COLLEEN: [*crying*] That'll be the bouquets—!
NAOMI: [*desperately trying to extract herself*] I'll get it!

> *She limps painfully to the door, desperate for a two second breather. Meanwhile* ANGELA *and* COLLEEN *resume buttoning up* MEG*'s dress.*

COLLEEN: Thank goodness. I was starting to worry. The florist told me they'd be here by eight—

> NAOMI *answers the door to an attractive man in his mid-thirties.* JAMES.

> *His eyes nearly pop out of his head when he sees* NAOMI *in the bridesmaid's dress.*

NAOMI: James!
JAMES: [*overlapping*] Naomi?!

MEG: James!
JAMES: [*recovering himself*] Naomi. Hi.
COLLEEN: James!
MEG: James! Thank God you're here!

> *She rushes over to her fiance, desperately in need of reassurance.* COLLEEN *follows, placing herself between them and trying to block James' view.*

COLLEEN: [*overlapping*] No, no, you shouldn't have come—!
JAMES: [*overlapping*] I got all your messages. What's wrong?
COLLEEN: [*overlapping*] It's bad luck for you to see Meg before the wedding!
MEG: M-u-u-u-m-!
COLLEEN: [*trying to push him out the door*] You can talk to her at the church—
MEG: No Mum. I need to talk to him *now*. Privately. *Then* I'll kick him out.
COLLEEN: All right, all right, but be quick. The photographer will be here soon. [*Then to* JAMES] And try not to look at her.
JAMES: I'll avert my eyes.
ANGELA: [*feeling sick for* MEG] Well, we'll wait next door then.
COLLEEN: Don't be too long.

> COLLEEN *exits, followed by* ANGELA. *Meanwhile* NAOMI *stands near* JAMES *and* MEG, *frozen with terror. A couple of beats, then* ANGELA *re-emerges, and—*

ANGELA: Naomi!
NAOMI: [*jumping*] Ohh!

> NAOMI *moves quickly past* JAMES *and* MEG *and limps from the room as fast as her incredibly painful shoes will take her.*

> MEG *and* JAMES *are alone. He looks at her warily. He's got a bad feeling. But he covers.*

JAMES: I'm not having much luck averting my eyes. You look beautiful.

> *In spite of everything,* MEG *can't help glowing a little at that.*

MEG: Do you think so?
JAMES: [*nodding, absolutely genuine*] You look amazing…

> MEG*'s pleased, but when he moves to touch her, she moves away.*

MEG: I didn't know you knew Naomi.
JAMES: Yeah, we met at that party, remember? So what's she doing here? And where's Lucy?
NAOMI: I kicked her out because she said you've been having an affair.
JAMES: What?!
MEG: She said you've been having an affair.
JAMES: What?! Where the hell did she get that from?
MEG: [*wanting desperately to believe this*] So it's not true?

> JAMES *hedges, desperate to avoid a blatant lie.*

JAMES: Meg, I love you. More than anything.
MEG: And you wouldn't cheat on me?
JAMES: I want to marry you, in case you hadn't noticed.

> *But* MEG *pushes, determined to get a direct answer.*

MEG: And you *promise* you've *never* cheated on me?

> *The tiniest hint of a pause, then...*

JAMES: No! No, of course I haven't. How could you think I'd—? No, Meg, absolutely not.

> MEG*'s face is initially a study in relief, but doubt quickly flickers over her features.*

MEG: I *want* to believe you...
JAMES: But you don't?
MEG: Well, Lucy's never lied to me yet.
JAMES: I guess Lucy must think it's true—God knows why—but she's wrong.

> MEG *stares up at him, studying his face for emotional details.*

She *is*. I promise you.

> *It's a struggle for* MEG *to believe him, and it shows. Another small silence, then...*

Meg, if you're going to believe some silly little rumour over my word, are you sure you *should* be marrying me?
MEG: Don't say that! I *want* to marry you!
JAMES: And I want to marry you too, but I need to know you trust me.
MEG: I do!
JAMES: Do you really?

MEG: Yes! Really! I do!
JAMES: You do?
MEG: I do.

> JAMES *smiles at her gently, warmly.*

JAMES: [*tenderly, teasing*] I like it when you say those two words...

> MEG *melts. He pursues the advantage and put his arms around her.*

Will you say them again in a couple of hours?
MEG: I might...
JAMES: Good... Is it bad luck to kiss the bride?
MEG: Who cares?

> *They fall into each other's arms and exchange a long kiss, then pull apart.*

JAMES: I love you, Meg.
MEG: I love you too.

> *Another deep smile between them, and then* JAMES *starts heading for the door.*

JAMES: We'll let them in, eh?

> MEG *nods. As* JAMES *turns and walks to the door, one look at his face shows how much he loathes himself right now. Meanwhile* MEG*'s ecstatic as she heads to the mirror. She's heard what she wants to hear and she's more than happy to believe it.*

You can come back now...

> *As* JAMES *opens the door and* COLLEEN, ANGELA *and* NAOMI *re-enter,* MEG *greets them with a beaming smile.* NAOMI *looks like she could crack at any second, but* MEG *is oblivious.*

MEG: Come on in, everything's fine!
COLLEEN: It's all sorted out then?
MEG: Yeah, Mum.
COLLEEN: Oh, lovely!
ANGELA: So everything's okay?
MEG: [*nodding*] It's perfect.

> ANGELA *is bemused, to say the least. How could they sort it out that quickly?*

ANGELA: Are you sure, Meg?
MEG: [*beaming*] Yeah, I'm sure.

> MEG *slips her arm through* JAMES' *arm and smiles at the stunned* NAOMI, *who is hovering behind* ANGELA.

[*To* NAOMI] We *did* have a bit of a drama, but we've talked it through and we've sorted it out.
JAMES: Yeah. Everything's fine.

> *He throws a barely perceptible look at* NAOMI, *which she misinterprets.*

COLLEEN: Oh, I'm so glad!
MEG: So let's get ready for a wedding, eh?
COLLEEN: Lovely! [*Grabbing* JAMES' *arm*] Now *you* have to leave, Young Man—

> *As* COLLEEN *starts leading* JAMES *to the door, a deeply emotional* NAOMI *approaches* MEG.

NAOMI: This is *really* beautiful! [*Crying*] You are *so* courageous…
MEG: [*bemused*] Ah… thanks…

> JAMES *has just realised that* NAOMI *is about to blow it. As he tries to 'casually' extricate himself from* COLLEEN *at the door—*

NAOMI: And you still want me to be your bridesmaid?
MEG: [*smiling, confused*] Of course. Why wouldn't I—?

> *But* JAMES *has made it back to* MEG'*s side in half a second flat.*

JAMES: [*interrupting*] You know, maybe you should just have one bridesmaid?!

> ANGELA *has just realised what's going on, and jumps in to try and help save the situation.*

ANGELA: That's what I suggested before. I don't think the dress looks good on her—
MEG: Angela!
JAMES: Look, I don't want to offend Naomi, but I agree. It looks sort of funny—
MEG: James—!
JAMES: What do you think, Colleen?
COLLEEN: [*worried*] I think it looks fine. You think it looks funny?
JAMES: [*darting* NAOMI *warning looks*] No offence Naomi, I know it's

rude to say this when I've only met you *once before*, but—

NAOMI *suddenly gets the message:* MEG *doesn't know.*

NAOMI: [*overlapping, sub-text*] Oh! Oh! Okay. Yeah. I think you're right. The colour's the problem.

COLLEEN: What's wrong with the colour?

NAOMI: It doesn't suit me.

MEG: Rubbish!

NAOMI: [*overlapping*] I think you'd better just have one bridesmaid.

MEG: No, I'm having *two!* I don't know what's got into these people, but I apologise for their rudeness. You look gorgeous. Doesn't she, Mum?

COLLEEN: Yes, beautiful. And besides, we don't have time to rearrange the bridal table.

Underneath all this, JAMES *and* NAOMI *have been communicating wordlessly.*

JAMES: All right, I've been told. I'm sorry if I offended you, Naomi.

MEG: I should think so. [*Gently pushing* JAMES] Now get out of here. We've got a wedding to get to.

JAMES: Consider me gone.

He starts to walk from the room, holding his hands in front of his eyes so he can't see.

JAMES: [*teasing*] See Colleen? Not looking.

COLLEEN: [*giggling girlishly*] Ohhh, James…

But as JAMES *passes* NAOMI, *he trips and loses his balance. She instinctively reaches out to steady him and they end up tangled in each other's arms, unwittingly embracing.*

JAMES: Ohh!

MEG: Careful!

NAOMI: Ohhh!

JAMES: Sorry! Sorry about that Naomi…

NAOMI *suddenly bursts into floods of tears as she meets* JAMES' *eyes.*

NAOMI: I can't do this!

JAMES: [*deliberately misunderstanding*] Of course you can. Forget what I said. The dress looks great—

He tries to free himself from her grasp but she's gripping him tightly.

NAOMI: No, I meant I can't do this anymore!

MEG *looks between* NAOMI *and* JAMES, *an awful thought forming.*

MEG: Do what?!

JAMES *manages to free himself and start heading for the door.*

JAMES: Nothing. I don't know. See you at the church—!

NAOMI: [*overlapping*] I've been having an affair with James! I'm so sorry!

COLLEEN *sinks into a chair, stunned.* MEG *stands transfixed. A long silence, then...*

MEG: Oh fuck...

MEG *lunges at* JAMES, *pummeling him with her fists.*

[*Yelling, crying*] You lying bastard! You lying fucking bastard!

JAMES: Meg—Meg—listen—!

MEG: [*to* NAOMI] Get out of here!

NAOMI: I'm so sorry—

MEG: [*yelling at* JAMES] And you—you get out of here too!!!

MEG *lunges towards* NAOMI *as though she's going to literally kick her out.*

Now!!! [*A thought occurs*] But don't go together! [*Another thought, to* JAMES] No, you stay!

NAOMI: [*trying to approach her*] I didn't mean for this to happen—!

MEG: [*yelling over her*] Get the dress off! Go on, take it off now! [*To* COLLEEN *and* ANGELA] Take it off her!

COLLEEN *and* ANGELA *descend on the sobbing* NAOMI *and very quickly relieve her of the bridesmaid's dress. Meanwhile—*

JAMES: Meg, I can explain everything—

MEG: I thought you already did! [*Yelling to* ANGELA *and* COLLEEN] And take those shiny shoes off her too!

She hurries to NAOMI, *who now only wears the expensive French underwear, and starts literally pushing her out the door.* NAOMI *has time to grab her handbag, but her clothes are left behind.*

[*To* JAMES] Nice underwear, isn't it? No doubt you've already seen it! [*Shoving* NAOMI *to the door*] Get out! Go on, get out—! And don't ever come near me again!

> NAOMI *runs out the door in her underwear.* MEG *slams it after her, then collapses on the bed, sobbing.* JAMES *kneels beside the bed as* COLLEEN *hurries to the other side.*

COLLEEN: Sweetheart... Oh, Sweetheart... [*Turning on* JAMES] Get out of here!

JAMES: Colleen, please—

COLLEEN: I said get out!

JAMES: I need to talk to Meg alone—

COLLEEN: I'm not leaving her alone with you. How could you do this to her?

JAMES: Can you just give us a few minutes—?

COLLEEN: You should be down on your knees thanking God you've got a girl like Meg, but *this* is how you behave—

JAMES: Please, Colleen. I need to explain it to her.

COLLEEN: You can't explain something like this. People will be arriving in an hour. Should I call your father and tell him to cancel—?

MEG: [*overlapping, sobbing*] Mum, just give us a few minutes. It's okay. I need to talk to him. Please.

> *As* COLLEEN *hovers reluctantly,* ANGELA *takes her arm.*

ANGELA: Come on, Mrs. Bacon...

> COLLEEN *shrugs* ANGELA *off, but reluctantly turns to leave. She looks daggers at* JAMES *as they pass. Perhaps* ANGELA*'s look contains the tiniest hint of empathy—but not much.*

COLLEEN: I'm ashamed of you.

ANGELA: Well, it was worth it, wasn't it? We'll be downstairs, Meg.

> ANGELA *and* COLLEEN *exit.*
>
> JAMES *looks at* MEG, *torn. What to say? How can he explain this?*

JAMES: Meg...Meg?

> MEG *puts a pillow over her head, refusing to hear him.* JAMES *hesitates a moment, then he turns towards the audience, filled with guilt, anger and loathing—all directed squarely at himself.*
>
> *Lights fade into:*

SCENE NINE

Spotlight on JAMES *as he addresses the audience, knowing they hate him as much as he hates himself right now, and trying in vain to explain the indefensible.*

JAMES: [*grasping at straws*] Look, sex and love are separate things... Well, they *can be,* that's all I'm saying. This thing with Naomi— okay, it should never have happened—but it didn't *have to* impact on what I have with Meg. I thought that was the deal. It was a *separate* arrangement. She told me she just wanted a bit of fun, and now she turns around and does *this...!* I mean, where the hell did that come from? If I'd known Naomi felt like that I would've broken it off with her months ago— [*A beat as he realises: Who is he kidding?*] Well, maybe. Oh shit, maybe not. But I just—I just— [*A short silence as he struggles with his confusion*] I just wish women would say what they mean. You know—plainly, clearly state what they want instead of expecting you to be psychic. Meg bought me this T-shirt at the Warner Brothers store, and it's got a picture of Superman on it. He's wearing this perplexed expression and he's saying *You want me to leap tall buildings and be sensitive and supportive?!* That's how it is with women. They want you to slay a dragon for them one second, then cry at a guide dog commercial the next. And somehow you're expected to guess when they want you to be controlling and when they want you to be crying—and if you don't make the right guess at the right time it's instantly construed as proof that you don't love them enough. *If you really loved me, you wouldn't need to ask.* How many times have I heard that? Well I'm sorry, I've loved a few people a lot, but no-one's ever stepped out of the shadows and handed me a crystal ball. [*Sighs, hates himself for making excuses*] Anyway, I know I'm trying to change the subject. The fact is, I've been acting like a prick.

Light's fade.

SCENE TEN

The door bursts open and NAOMI *re-enters in a hotel bathrobe. In tears and clutching soggy tissues, she addresses the audience directly.*

NAOMI: I had to walk down to reception in my undies, because I was too scared to go back in there and ask for my clothes! And you know what? Even though I felt so guilty and so ashamed, I still found myself thinking 'thank God I didn't wear that old blue bra and the baggy cottontails'. Does that make me a bad person? Oh, I don't know. Maybe I already was... When I was younger I never thought I'd have an affair with *anyone's* boyfriend... let alone a friend's boyfriend... let alone a friend's *fiance*... But things seem really simple when you're young—everything's so black and white. But as soon as life gets interesting it starts to turn to grey. I didn't know he was Meg's fiance when I met him... I was drunk and he was cute and what happened happened... and then I found out he was getting married, but I really liked him by then. I tried to end it but... well, I didn't... and I kind of convinced myself—and him—that it was cool, that I could handle it, I just wanted some fun with no strings attached... and then, well, then I got Meg's wedding invitation— and that's how I found out it was him! [*Pause as she remembers the awful moment*] Can you *believe* it? *I* couldn't. I just, I didn't know what to do, and... [*Looks at the audience guiltily*] Oh look, I know what you're thinking. I shouldn't have accepted the invitation. And maybe I shouldn't have. But I couldn't help it. I wanted James to look around the church and see my face and feel like the bastard he was—at least, that's what I told myself. But when he ended things two weeks ago I realised I'd been secretly hoping that when it came to the crunch he'd say to the priest 'I can't go through with this. The woman I *really* love is sitting over there!' Dumb fantasy, huh? And awful to Meg. Sometimes I look at myself in the mirror and think 'With friends like me, who needs enemies?' But you know how sometimes when you need it most you can't get your head and your heart to co-operate? Well, I hated what me and James were doing— in my head—but still, I couldn't seem to kick him out of my bed.

Lights fade.

SCENE ELEVEN

Lights up. JAMES *and* MEG *are alone now. He looks down at her on the bed, head covered by a pillow, and moves towards her helplessly. How to explain the unjustifiable? He doesn't know how he'll do it, all he knows is he has to do it, or he'll lose her.*

JAMES: I'm *so* sorry I lied… I panicked, Meg… I love you so much and I was scared I'd lose you…
MEG: [*from under the pillow*] That's not good enough.
JAMES: [*ashamed*] I know…

> *He waits for another reaction, but nothing comes. He moves closer to the bed.*

I just… I can't tell you how sorry I am… I never meant for this to happen.
MEG: [*emerging from behind the pillow*] Oh, so it was an accident?
JAMES: [*grabbing at this*] Well, yeah. In a way it was.
MEG: What? Your zip fell open and gravity got the better of Naomi's undies and you tripped and your dick fell into her?

> *There's no answer to that.* JAMES *ploughs on.*

JAMES: It was that weekend you went to see Lynne. I was out with—
MEG: [*interrupting*] In *April?*

> *An intensely awkward silence as his nod confirms this. April was five whole months ago.*

JAMES: Yeah—I went to the pub with Tom, and we got talking to Naomi and some other girl. I didn't even know she knew you—

> *The second this is out,* JAMES *realises what a misjudged excuse it is.* MEG's *icy stare confirms it. He quickly tries to dig himself out of the hole that keeps deepening.*

[*Hastily*] Anyway—I was having a shit of a time at work—that was when the Optus thing was going on, remember? And you'd been so busy with work and uni and organising the wedding with your mum and I just, I was missing you already, and then you told me you were going away—

> *Against all her better judgement,* MEG *feels guilty.*

MEG: Oh, for a *weekend*.
JAMES: Yeah, but—I need you, Meg. I need you to be with me.
MEG: I am. I'm always there for you. You know that.
JAMES: I needed you *then*.
MEG: [*a flash of fury*] So it's *my* fault *you* fucked someone else?
JAMES: No, no, of course not. That's not what I'm saying.
MEG: Just as well. Keep going.
JAMES: Well, like I said, I was missing you and—

> *But in spite of herself,* MEG's *still feeling guilty.*

MEG: [*interjecting, guiltily*] I wasn't that busy—
JAMES: [*overlapping*]—and I got a bit pissed, and then we went on to a nightclub with Naomi and her girlfriend and we had a few more—
MEG: [*interrupting coldly*] Which nightclub?
JAMES: [*thrown*] What?
MEG: Which nightclub did you go to?
JAMES: I can't remember. Heat, maybe—
MEG: [*disgusted*] At the casino?
JAMES: [*embarrassed*] Tom had free passes. Anyway— [*Struggling to continue*] We had some more drinks, and it got late, and then me and Naomi shared a taxi... and somehow we ended up at her place—
MEG: Somehow?
JAMES: Yeah. I was pissed, Meg. I wasn't thinking straight. I know that's not much of an excuse but... anyway, we went upstairs and... next thing I knew... well, we started—

> MEG *interrupts, hands over her ears.*

MEG: Stop! Don't tell me anymore.
JAMES: Okay, fine.
MEG: No tell me.
JAMES: Are you sure?
MEG: [*nodding, wincing*] Yes. I want to know.
JAMES: You don't look like you want to know.
MEG: No I do want to know. Tell me.

> *Another beat of silence.* JAMES *looks uncertain about whether to continue.*

Go on. Go.
JAMES: [*deeply uncomfortable*] Well, I was drunk, I was missing you, it

was out of my control, Meg—and before I knew it we were—
MEG: [*interrupting*] Stop!

    JAMES *stops, relieved, then almost straight away—*

No, go on. No, go.
JAMES: [*he hates saying this*] Well, we ended up in bed.

    MEG *visibly winces.* JAMES *tries to touch her hand. She pulls away sharply.*

But it didn't mean anything, Meg—
MEG: Did you go down on her?
JAMES: What—?
MEG: Don't answer that question!
JAMES: I woke up the next morning and I hated myself. I loved *you*—
MEG: [*overlapping, another blow*] You woke up? So you stayed the night?
JAMES: [*oops*] Well, yeah—but only because I was too drunk to—
MEG: [*interrupting*] And did you do it again in the morning?
JAMES: No! No way! I couldn't get out of there fast enough. And all I could think about all weekend was seeing you again.
MEG: [*remembering*] You met me at the airport with flowers…

    The memory that will have to be revised with unwelcome new knowledge hangs in the air for a moment.

And I thought it was just because you loved me…
JAMES: It was. [*Beat*] Mostly.

    MEG *forces herself back to the present. Her anger takes over again.*

MEG: All right, that might explain once, but Lucy said it went on for *months*.
JAMES: Well, yeah, it did… sort of…
MEG: Sort of? What—you were *sort of* fucking her on a regular basis?
JAMES: I know how it sounds, but it was out of my control—
MEG: Oh, give me a break.
JAMES: [*overlapping*] After it happened the first time, I put it out of my mind. It was a one-off as far as I was concerned—But then Naomi started ringing me at work—and she turned up one day and asked if I could go for coffee. She'd just broken-up with her boyfriend. I felt sorry for her.

MEG: So you screwed her as an act of charity? What a great guy.

>JAMES *kicks himself internally. With every attempt at an explanation, he seems to be making things worse.*

JAMES: That's not what I'm saying. I just… I didn't know how to get out of it… And I didn't want to hurt her feelings.

MEG: Hers? What about *mine..?*

>*Her anger evaporates into tears.* JAMES *hates seeing her in such pain. He tries to move closer, but she steps away.*

JAMES: See, this is why I didn't tell you… I couldn't bear to see you so hurt… And I thought it'd all just sort itself out.

MEG: How? How can something like this just sort itself out?

JAMES: [*knowing this is lame*] I don't know… I thought the honeymoon's for six weeks, she'll get over it while we're away…

MEG: If you really thought that, then you're a moron as well as an arsehole. And you're a coward too.

JAMES: Fair enough. I don't blame you for thinking that. I'm just glad the truth's out.

MEG: Really?

JAMES: Yeah. I hate lying to you. It's been horrendous for me.

MEG: But somehow you've managed it. As recently as ten minutes ago, in fact.

JAMES: I'm sorry about that, I panicked—

MEG: [*overlapping*] How many times did you have sex?

JAMES: Meg… don't…

MEG: How many?

JAMES: [*after a beat*] Three or four.

MEG: Bullshit.

JAMES: Five or six. It doesn't matter, Meg. It didn't mean anything.

MEG: It looked like it meant something to her.

JAMES: She knew I loved you. She knew we were getting married—

MEG: [*overlapping*] She's got a good body, hasn't she?

JAMES: What—?

MEG: She hasn't got flab on her tummy like I have.

JAMES: Meg, you're beautiful—

MEG: [*overlapping*] She's firm. She's got a great body, hasn't she?

JAMES: Why are you doing this to yourself?

MEG: Just answer the question.

    JAMES *knows he can't win here, but answers anyway.*
JAMES: I think her body's average.
MEG: Then why did you sleep with her?

    As JAMES *searches for the right answer...*
Because you could.

    His silence confirms this. She snorts with derision.
God, what is it with men? Don't you have any willpower, or principles?

    JAMES *can't hold in his defensiveness much longer.*
JAMES: Come on... You're not going to start on that 'all men are bastards' stuff—?
MEG: No, not all men. Only you.

    JAMES *bites back a defensive response, then...*
JAMES: Meg, I want to marry you. Doesn't that count for anything?
MEG: [*genuinely trying to understand*] But... if you really want to be with me forever, why would you do something like this?
JAMES: *Because* I want to be with you forever. *Because* I take marriage so seriously. In a weird way, that's exactly why.
MEG: How do you work *that* out?
JAMES: Look, I want to wake up with you every morning for the rest of my life. I've got no doubts about that. None whatsoever. And that's a great thing to feel, but I'll be honest Meg, on one level I think it's been scaring the shit out of me too.
MEG: But why?
JAMES: Because I'm staring down the barrel of the fact that I'll never see another woman naked.

    MEG*'s not sure how to react. He feels like a heel.*
Okay, that sounds terrible—but it's scary to love someone so much that you never want to be with anyone else—and so, I guess this... opportunity... came up unexpectedly... and I suppose it was a bit like, well, I'll say goodbye to singlehood with this final, stupid fling...

    MEG *just stares at him, not knowing what to think.*
And that's all it ever was, Meg, a fling.
MEG: But... I need to be the only one.

JAMES: You *are*. You're the only woman I want. This... this stupid thing... it was just a mistake. It *never* changed how I feel about *you*.
MEG: But how can you say that? If I'm the only woman you want, you shouldn't *want* anyone else.
JAMES: Meg, you're my soul mate. That was just sex.
MEG: *Just* sex?
JAMES: Yes. Just sex. And we've got so much more than that.
MEG: But haven't we got *that*, too? Isn't our sex good enough for you?
JAMES: Of course it is! It's beautiful! *You're* beautiful. And I love you more than anything. But...

His voice trails off. MEG *misinterprets the pause.*

MEG: But you want to have sex with other people?
JAMES: No! That's not what I'm saying, but... it's just... if you want me to promise that I'll never find anyone else attractive, I can't do that—
MEG: I know. I know that. But—
JAMES: [*overlapping*] Can you promise me that you'll never be attracted to another man?
MEG: Of course not—
JAMES: And can you promise that you'll never be *tempted* to have an affair?
MEG: I can promise that I won't act on it.
JAMES: Can you? Can you really?
MEG: Yes I can.
JAMES: [*lowering his voice*] Meg, even *Angela's* had an affair.
MEG: Ssssh! I wasn't supposed to tell you that!
JAMES: She can't hear us.

MEG *looks thoughtful, anxious, tied up in knots.*

MEG: [*after a beat*] I don't like the way this is heading... Finding other people attractive's one thing, but... I have to know you're faithful, James. I need you to *promise me* this won't happen again.

JAMES *sighs, thinks for a moment, then decides to be courageously honest—at great risk.*

JAMES: It would be so easy for me to say 'I promise I'll be faithful forever, Meg'—but I've told you enough lies, and I don't want to do that anymore. I *can't* promise that I'll never do it again—

> MEG *gasps. That's really painful.*

[*Gently*] But I *can* promise that I don't *intend* to ever do it again, and I'll try with all my heart *not* to do it, and I'll always remember how important this is to you, and try to put your feelings first…

> MEG's *shell-shocked. She doesn't know what to say. He touches her gently.*

And I'm not going to ask *you* to promise *me* any more than that either, because… I know how these things can happen…

> MEG *is quiet, confused. She has no idea how to react. He strokes her hand silently.*

I'm not saying it *will* happen—I really don't think so—but I won't risk lying to you again…

> MEG's *silent, thinking, thinking… A beat or two, then…*

[*Tenderly, tentatively*] Meg..? What are you thinking..?

MEG: I just want you to be the same person you were yesterday.

JAMES: I am. I'm exactly the same guy. [*Gently touching her face*] I'll get down on my knees and apologise to you every day for the rest of my life if I have to.

MEG: Really?

JAMES: [*nodding, one hundred per cent sincere*] Really.

MEG: On one knee, or two?

JAMES: Left, right, one knee, two knees, whichever you like. And when my joints are old and crippled with arthritis, I'll write *I'm sorry* in the sand with my wheelchair.

> MEG *smiles in spite of herself.* JAMES *gets down on one knee. He takes both her hands.*

I'm deeply, deeply sorry Meg. This is something that should never have happened, and lying when you asked me was unforgivable. I'll never, ever lie to you again. I promise you that with all my heart.

> *They stare at each other. He takes both her hands.*

Now, while I'm down here… I can't help noticing that you seem to be dressed for an important appointment…

> MEG *smiles sadly, looks down at her now crumpled wedding dress.*
> JAMES *gently pulls her down onto the floor in front of him.*

Will you marry me?

MEG *thinks for a long moment, then...*

MEG: I might...

JAMES *is hurt, but he nods, accepting that she needs some time to make her decision.*

JAMES: I'll spend the rest of my life trying to make you happy, Meg, if you'll let me.... [*He kisses her gently, they pull apart*] I guess I'd better go, and give you some time...

He gets up and walks to the door, turning as he gets there.

I love you.

MEG: I know you do.

JAMES *smiles sadly and exits.* MEG *is still for a moment, then turns and meets the audience's eyes. Lights start to fade as we move into...*

SCENE TWELVE

MEG *addresses the audience directly.*

MEG: I blame Mum for this. I learned denial from her. She's a fantastic teacher. She gave me detailed, intricate lessons without one spoken word passing between us—which was, of course, the entire point. [*Beat*] Oh, I'm not stupid. I've had a kind of niggling feeling about James ... but I pushed it down from my brain and through my chest—carefully avoiding the heart area—and I kept pushing it down through my stomach and even further down still, until it was in the soles of my feet and every step I took squashed it. And when you've put in that kind of effort you don't want to be told it's in vain. Who wants to hear that the man they adore—the man they're about to commit their life to—has been having sex with somebody else? [*Gestures at the dress*] Who wants to put on this amazing, magical dress and then have to take it straight off again and zip it back up in its plastic? Who wants to be thirty-three years old—with a biological clock that ticks so loudly it keeps you awake at night, and back in the singles wilderness? Not me... [*A beat or two. She sighs, retreats back into flippancy*] This wasn't part of the fairytale, you know? Prince

Charming never did this to Cinderella. But then, this is the real world, isn't it? Well you know what I think? I think the real world sucks sometimes. I hate it. And you know what else— [*Beat, deeply angry*] I hate *them* too. I hate all of them. I do. I hate Naomi for betraying me, I hate Lucy for telling me, I hate Ange for not telling me, I hate James for cheating on me, then lying about it, and most of all for being honest, and I hate Mum for—well, I just hate her. [*Beat*] But I hate myself the most. I hate that I was so gutless that I ignored my instincts. And I hate the fact that if I had the chance, I'd probably do it again. [*Beat*] I don't want to know about this. It hurts too much. Things aren't what I thought. James isn't *who* I thought. There are bits of him I didn't know about, bits that break my heart in half... Do I have to learn to love those bits, too?

Lights fade as we move straight into...

SCENE THIRTEEN

MEG *wipes her eyes and blows her nose with an air of frenzied urgency. The clock's ticking. There's no time for contemplation and she feels compelled to make a quick decision. She starts fiddling frantically with her wedding dress as the door opens and* COLLEEN *enters with a tentative smile. She's nervous, uncertain.*

COLLEEN: Sweetheart? I just saw James leave. Is everything sorted out?
MEG: [*frenzied, fragile*] Yeah it is.
COLLEEN: Are you sure?
MEG: Yeah. I'm sure.
COLLEEN: Really?
MEG: [*shortly*] I just said so, didn't I Mum?
COLLEEN: [*happily, briskly*] All right, then! Well, let's get moving. Now Angela's gone down to pick up the flowers, and your father and the photographer will be here any minute, so we'd better get you into your veil—

COLLEEN *starts walking briskly to the wardrobe and gets* MEG*'s veil out.* MEG *stays still as her mother unzips the veil from its cover.*

Come on Sweetheart, quick sticks. [*Starting to take the veil out*] Look at this beautiful—Oh no!

MEG: What?!
COLLEEN: It's gone all limp—!
MEG: What do you mean?!
COLLEEN: [*fussing with the veil*] It's not as full as it was when we picked it up!
MEG: [*crumpling into tears*] Have I got a flat veil?

>COLLEEN *quickly realises her mistake. She's determinedly chirpy.*

COLLEEN: No, no, no! It's lovely, it's perfect. No, looking at it again, I was wrong. It's just right. And all we have to do is fluff it up, anyway. Sweetheart, don't cry. You'll have red eyes at your wedding.
MEG: [*sniffling*] I've got some Visine.

>MEG *is wiping away her tears with her hands.* COLLEEN *grabs a tissue and wipes her face, then holds it under her nose like she's a little girl.*

COLLEEN: Oh Sweetheart, come on... the veil looks beautiful... [*Holding the tissue under* MEG*'s nose*] Here. Blow...
MEG *does so.* COLLEEN *wipes her nose.*
Good girl.
She throws the tissues away.
Now let's put this on... All right?
MEG: [*nodding, sniffling*] All right.

>MEG *still sniffles as* COLLEEN *places the veil on her head. It has no floral headpiece yet.*

COLLEEN: Sit still... Here we are... Ohh, lovely...
MEG: Does it looks awful without the flowers?

>MEG *starts heading for the mirror on the other side of the room.* COLLEEN *follows, all hustle and bustle.*

COLLEEN: Angela will have the flowers up here any second—Oh, I keep forgetting to tell you—now the disco man rang yesterday and said that the Selena Dion song—the one from 'Titanic', with the—
MEG: [*overlapping*] Celine, Mum.
COLLEEN: What?
MEG: Her name's Celine.
COLLEEN: All right, whatever you like. Anyway, he thought he'd play that song when you're all entering instead of after the speeches, because that would fit in better with the other songs you were wanting.

I said I thought that'd be fine, but I'd have to check with you too, of course, so what do you— [think?]

> *But* MEG *can't take her mother's denial anymore. She snaps.*

MEG: [*interrupting*] How can you do this?
COLLEEN: What? Do what?
MEG: How can you just pretend that nothing's wrong? Didn't you *hear* what Naomi said?
COLLEEN: [*flustered*] Yes Sweetheart, of course I heard...
MEG: James has been having an affair! Don't you even *care?*

> *Poor* COLLEEN *doesn't know what to do. She's just been trying to do the right thing.*

COLLEEN: Of course I care, but you just told me everything was sorted out and I didn't want to spoil your day—
MEG: No Mum, you didn't want to spoil *your* day!
COLLEEN: Meg...
MEG: This whole thing's all about what *you* want, Mum. It's got nothing to do with me. All *I* have to do is turn up!

> COLLEEN *starts, looks deeply injured. Her thoughts fly swiftly back to her own wedding. She takes a moment, then takes* MEG*'s hands.*

COLLEEN: Oh Sweetheart, I'm sorry... I didn't mean to take over...
MEG: [*sniffling*] I know how much you've been looking forward to this. I don't want to let you down...

> COLLEEN *pulls* MEG *into a hug.* MEG *cries on her mother's shoulder.* COLLEEN *strokes her. In spite of her wedding mania the bottom line is, she loves* MEG *more.*

COLLEEN: Oh Sweetheart, you wouldn't be letting me down... [*A few beats of silence*] I was just trying to make things easier for everyone... and I did want your wedding day to be lovely, but I don't care about that if it's not what you want... I love you, Meg... I just want you to be happy... and if you think you should call it off, that's exactly what we'll do.
MEG: Do you mean that?
COLLEEN: Of course I do. If you don't want to marry James, I don't want you to either...

MEG *smiles at her mother, filled with love. They go into a warm hug.* COLLEEN *strokes* MEG *maternally. A few seconds pass. Then* COLLEEN *can't resist looking at her watch.*

But you *will* need to make up your mind fairly quickly.

The door opens and ANGELA *re-enters with the flowers. She looks uncertain. Is there going to be a wedding or isn't there?*

ANGELA: Ah, the flowers..?
COLLEEN: I'm not sure if we'll be needing them, Angela...
MEG: Yes, we will. We'll be needing them.
COLLEEN: Are you sure, Sweetheart?
MEG: Yeah, I *am* this time. I love him. I want to marry him.
COLLEEN: Are you certain about this?
MEG: [*nodding*] Positive.
ANGELA: You don't *have to* go through with it, Meg.
MEG: I know I don't have to, but I *want* to.

It's said with such certainty that COLLEEN *and* ANGELA *are completely convinced.*

COLLEEN: [*smiling*] All right, then! [*Getting to her feet*] We'd better get that headpiece on in a hurry.

ANGELA *takes* MEG'*s floral headpiece out of the box. Ad-lib favourable reactions. Then they attach it (it's on a slide comb) to the front of* MEG'*s veil.*

Just bend your head down for a moment Meg, that's right... now, Angela... just—gently—slide it into there... that's right... [*etc*]

MEG: Has she gone?
ANGELA: Who?
MEG: You know who I mean. Has she gone?
ANGELA: [*nodding*] She's well and truly gone, Meg.
MEG: I just need to know she's not here.
COLLEEN: She's not here.

The phone rings. ANGELA *moves over to answer it while* COLLEEN *fluffs up* MEG'*s veil.*

ANGELA: [*into the phone*] Hello? Oh, hi, Mr. Bacon, yeah it's Angela. Great. Yeah, okay. We'll be right down. Bye.

She hangs up.

Your dad's here, and the photographer's setting up down in the courtyard.

They all start rushing even more. As COLLEEN *hurries to the cupboard to get her coat—*

COLLEEN: Good! Angela, could you grab Meg's bouquet—?

MEG: [*overlapping*] I've got to fix my makeup first! I look awful!

COLLEEN: You look beautiful!

MEG: I'm a mess, Mum! You two go first. [*As they hesitate*] Go on. Get the bridesmaid and the parents shots. I'll be down in a minute.

COLLEEN: Are you sure?

MEG: [*nodding, putting on a shoe*] I've got to find the Visine and put on my shoes—

Meanwhile ANGELA *has been pinning* COLLEEN*'s corsage on her coat. She pricks her.*

COLLEEN: Oww! You go, Angela. I don't want to leave Meg alone—

MEG: [*all smiles*] Mum I'm fine, I'm great, I'm getting married in forty minutes and at this rate we're not going to make it to the church.

COLLEEN: [*thrilled*] All right then! [*Fiddling with her hair in the mirror*] We'll see you downstairs—out in the courtyard—five minutes?

MEG: *Three* minutes. Oh, and you both look gorgeous.

ANGELA *and* COLLEEN *smile at the compliment.*

ANGELA: So do you, Meg. You look beautiful.

MEG *gives a hollow half-laugh. She feels anything but beautiful right now.*

MEG: Yeah, right…

COLLEEN: [*teary*] You *do* Sweetheart. You look like an angel… [*Then suddenly bossy*] Come on Angela, quickly!

ANGELA *and* COLLEEN *exit.*

Left alone, MEG *grabs a full champagne glass in a frenzy and drinks it all in one gulp. Then she frantically searches for her other wedding shoe, only to realise she's holding it in her hand. She hurriedly tries to put on the buckled shoe, tripping over her heavy dress and having to try the delicate operation from several different angles. Her air of frenzied urgency only makes it more difficult. She then searches through her makeup bag for the Visine, only to accidentally spill the bag's entire contents on the bed. She groans and anxiously rifles through the cosmetics to find the Visine. She grabs it, perches on the edge of the bed and leans back, applying a few drops to each eye. It stings.*

MEG: Ouch... ooh...

She sits still, eyes closed, head tilted back, face pointing up towards the ceiling, waiting for the drops to take effect, as—

The door opens and LUCY *enters.*

She stops in surprise as she sees MEG *sitting on the edge of the bed in her full bridal regalia. She's thinking about whether to turn and leave when—*

[*With her eyes closed*] I said I'd be down in a— [*Opening her eyes, she sees* LUCY] Oh. It's you.

LUCY: I thought you'd be gone by now. I came to get my stuff. I'll go.

MEG: It's all right. You can get your stuff.

LUCY *nods defiantly and starts walking across the room to the bathroom.*

[*Coldly*] And then go.

LUCY: [*colder*] Right.

LUCY *goes into the bathroom to get her toiletries bag. Meanwhile* MEG *starts applying makeup in a self-conscious frenzy. She's anxious to appear indifferent to* LUCY*'s presence, but her air of indifference is palpably manufactured.*

LUCY *emerges from the bathroom with her stuff and walks all the way across the room to the door. She's about to leave, when...*

MEG: It was true, Lucy. What you said.

LUCY: I know. I'm sorry.

MEG *gestures towards her bridal regalia.*

MEG: I s'pose you think I'm stupid?

LUCY: I don't know. What the hell would I know? I just wanted you to have all the information.

MEG: [*dryly*] Yeah, well, thanks for that.

> *An awkward silence. As* LUCY *hovers in the doorway, preparing to leave...*

You can... hang around for a few minutes if you want...
LUCY: Do you want me to?
MEG: Do *you* want to?
LUCY: It depends on what *you* want, Meg.

> *In spite of herself,* MEG *feels her ready sense of humour rising to the surface.*

MEG: I would've thought it was pretty obvious that I don't know *what* the hell I want right now.
LUCY: Yeah... Fair enough...
MEG: You'll have to decide.
LUCY: Okay, then. I'll stay.

> MEG *is clearly pleased. She starts sliding to one side of the bed, moving her dress to make room for* LUCY. LUCY *smiles and comes to sit beside her. Silence for a moment, then...*

Can I help you with anything?

> *Then, in spite of the overwhelming awfulness of the situation,* MEG *can't resist sharing something ironic with her best friend.*

MEG: You know, I asked Naomi Bartlett to take your place.
LUCY: What?!
MEG: [*nodding*] I asked her to be my bridesmaid.
LUCY: You didn't?!
MEG: Yes I did.

> LUCY*'s instant reaction is a grin. She quickly stifles it, feeling guilty. But* MEG *is grinning too. And she's starting to giggle, though her mirth has a manic edge.*

LUCY: You're kidding?!
MEG: [*giggling*] Can you believe it? She had the dress on when I found out...
LUCY: Oh my God...
MEG: Mum even put toilet paper in the toes of your shoes..!
LUCY: [*laughing openly*] Oh my God..!
MEG: [*laughing*] And when I found out we took the dress off her and she had to leave the hotel in her undies...!

LUCY: Oh, Meg..!
MEG: [*giggling*] God, why am I laughing? I can't believe I'm laughing. I must be hysterical... [*Wiping tears of laughter away*] Shit. Now I've stuffed up my makeup again...
LUCY: [*tentatively*] Do you want me to fix it?
MEG: Yeah, okay.

> LUCY *comes over and starts doing* MEG*'s makeup for her.*

[*Grinning*] You know the story... Slap it on three inches thick but make it look like I'm not wearing any.
LUCY: Don't talk. Your foundation will crack.

> LUCY *applies powder foundation to* MEG*'s face.*

Okay... Let's just smooth it in a bit...

> MEG *grabs* LUCY*'s arm in a sudden, urgent action—*

MEG: Lucy, what am I going to do? Should I marry him?
LUCY: I don't know, Meg. Do you want to?
MEG: Yes. No. I don't know. [*Beat. She sighs*] He said that he can't promise me he'll never do it again. He can promise he'll try really hard, but he can't promise for certain that he won't.
LUCY: Well, at least he's respecting you enough to be honest.
MEG: Yeah, I guess we both know where we stand now... Mind you, I thought we did before...

> *Another silence.* LUCY *touches her sympathetically.*

Lucy, do you reckon *you* could be faithful to someone for the rest of your life?
LUCY: I'm probably the wrong person to ask.
MEG: Probably.

> *They share a grin, then* MEG*'s grin disappears as she grapples with reality again.*

God, I just—I want to marry him but I *don't* as well.

> LUCY *knows instinctively that* MEG *needs her to take control.*

LUCY: Well, how about we finish this for starters, [*the makeup*] so you can keep your options open?
MEG: [*nodding*] Okay...

> LUCY *gets two blushers out of* MEG*'s makeup bag.*

LUCY: Now, what blusher would madam like to wear? *Burnished Rose*, or *Autumn Sunset?*
MEG: I told you I'm incapable of decisions right now.
LUCY: Okay. *Autumn Sunset* then—
MEG: [*overlapping, decisive*] No, *Burnished Rose*.
LUCY: [*grinning*] Right. *Burnished Rose* it is.

> *She starts to apply it to* MEG'*s cheeks.*

MEG: And just a little bit. I don't want to look like a clown.
LUCY: Oh, really? You're such a killjoy.
MEG: [*dryly*] Ha. Look who's talking.

> *They grin at each other,* LUCY *a little ruefully.*

LUCY: Guess I asked for that one, didn't I?

> *They smile at each other again, then* MEG *suddenly feels a burst of emotion.*

MEG: But seriously Luce… thanks for telling me… It took a lot of guts…
LUCY: Keep still. Do you want *Burnished Rose* all over your nose?

> MEG *suddenly grabs* LUCY *and hugs her tight.* LUCY *hugs her back.*

MEG: You're such a good friend…
LUCY: So are you.

> *They're wrapped in each other's embrace for a moment, then, as they pull apart…*

LUCY: Want to pash?

> MEG *laughs and playfully pushes her away.*

MEG: Shut-up!

> *They both grin. Then, after another short silence…*

   Who *did* you pash, Lucy?
LUCY: If I told you, you wouldn't believe me.
MEG: Oh come on. I'd believe *anything* from *you*. Who was it?
LUCY: You really want to know?
MEG: I'm *dying* to know.
LUCY: Are you sure?
MEG: Just tell me!
LUCY: [*grinning*] Naomi.

MEG: What?!
LUCY: [*laughing*] It was Naomi Bartlett.
MEG: Oh my God!

> *She gapes at* LUCY. *Then they both fall about giggling and laughing.*

LUCY: She's *anybody's*.

THE END

It's My Party (And I'll Die If I Want To)

It's My Party (And I'll Die If I Want To) was first performed at La Mama Theatre, Carlton, in conjunction with the Melbourne Comedy Festival, on 31 March 1993 with the following cast:

RON PATTERSON	Jim Daly
MICHAEL PATTERSON	Leon Teague
DEBBIE PATTERSON	Helen Rollinson
KAREN PATTERSON	Sarah Walker
DAWN PATTERSON	Libby Stone
TED WILKINS	Adriano Cortese

Dramaturg / Director, Catherine Hill
Designer, Linley Kensitt
Lighting Designer, Andrew Livingston
Stage Manager, Stacey Moulday

CHARACTERS

RON PATTERSON, sixtyish, robust, decisive, patriarchal
DAWN PATTERSON, sixtyish, warm, lovable, surprisingly astute
MICHAEL PATTERSON, thirty-six, tense, image-conscious, driven
DEBBIE PATTERSON, thirty-two, creative, fun, vulnerable
KAREN PATTERSON, twenty-four, spoilt, self-absorbed, petulant
TED WILKINS, twenty-five, polite, personable, eager-to-please

ACT ONE

The stage is in darkness.

Through the blackness we hear the loud ticking of a clock.

A few seconds tick away. Then the ticking fades out as a spotlight comes up.

A man, aged about sixty, dressed in an old-fashioned but immaculately neat suit stands in the spotlight beneath a round clock. The man is RON PATTERSON. *The clock is on the wall of his living room. It reads 8.34pm. The living room is a study in beige suburbia. On one end of a cabinet sits a sizeable and intricately detailed model of the* HMS Bounty *that* RON *has laboured over for many hours. A white sheet hangs on one wall and a slide projector is set up nearby. On the table are plates of Saladas with cheese and asparagus, cocktail frankfurts and sausage rolls.*

RON: [*direct to audience*] Good evening. At ten twenty-three pm on January twenty-four my doctor gave me three months to live. By my calculations, that leaves me with exactly… [*Looks at clock.*] one hundred and eleven minutes. So Dawn's invited the kids around for sausage rolls and Saladas.

    Fade to black.

    The clock ticks loudly for a few seconds. Lights up.

    DEBBIE *is sitting on the lounge flicking through Dawn's* Woman's Weekly. *She wears a tailored but slightly left-of-centre pantsuit and has an air of tight control. Her brother* MICHAEL *is hovering tensely near the table. He wears a suit.*

MICHAEL: Saladas and sausage rolls. They've got to be kidding.

    DEBBIE *doesn't respond.* MICHAEL *looks at his watch. He bites into a sausage roll, then discards it in disgust.*

I have to be somewhere. How long's this going to take?

DEBBIE: [*turning a page*] I don't know any more than you do, Michael.
MICHAEL: This is so typical. Isn't it? Isn't it?

    DEBBIE *doesn't respond.*

He clicks his fingers and we come running. No. No. He doesn't click *his*. That'd entail a bit of effort. He gets someone else to click theirs for him. Who rang you?
DEBBIE: Mum.
MICHAEL: [*overlapping, this proves his point*] That'd be right. And what did she say?
DEBBIE: [*doesn't want to get drawn into this*] She said, 'Dad wants you at our house tonight. It's very important'.
MICHAEL: My secretary told me.
DEBBIE: Your *secretary?!*
MICHAEL: Well, admittedly Mum tried to get through a few times. But I've had a lot of meetings.
DEBBIE: Michael.
MICHAEL: I would have called her back. I was waiting for the London Exchange to close.
DEBBIE: [*shaking her head*] You're going to work yourself into an early grave. You know that, don't you?
MICHAEL: Deb. Don't start—
DEBBIE: [*overlapping*] Well have you looked in a mirror lately? You look about fifty.
MICHAEL: I looked twenty years younger before I left the office. It's coming *home* that ages me.
DEBBIE: You let it get to you too much. Just... try thinking tranquil thoughts. And take a few deep breaths... from your diaphragm...

    MICHAEL'*s looking at her like she's gone mad.*

MICHAEL: Spare me the yoga lessons, Deb. You hate being here as much as I do.
DEBBIE: Not anymore. I'm completely relaxed.
MICHAEL: You're completely relaxed?
DEBBIE: [*nodding*] Coming home causes me no stress at all.
MICHAEL: May I remind you last time we were here I had to restrain you from braining Dad with *The Bounty*?
DEBBIE: I'd had a bad day.

MICHAEL *looks unconvinced.*

Well I've been giving this whole issue some serious thought… and the thing is… Dad's not going to change, so *I* am. Water off a duck's back, Michael. I'm not going to let him get to me anymore.

MICHAEL: [*scoffing*] Yeah, right.

DEBBIE: [*overlapping*] You're not going to drag me into this. Just because *you* don't have the nerve to tell them the truth—

MICHAEL: [*overlapping*] Debbie not now. Please. I just—*not now*, all right?

DEBBIE *stops and looks at him more closely. His distress is genuine. Her tone becomes gentler.*

DEBBIE: What is it, Michael? What's wrong with you tonight?

MICHAEL *sighs. He leans forward conspiratorially.*

MICHAEL: Do you remember last Christmas?

DEBBIE: What about it?

MICHAEL: Monique loaned Mum her silver salad servers.

DEBBIE: So…?

MICHAEL: So… she's coming 'round tomorrow to pick them up.

The way MICHAEL *delivers this, it is obviously highly significant.*

DEBBIE: Well. It had to happen. You couldn't keep them apart forever.

MICHAEL: You know what this means, don't you Debbie? It means I have to tell them *tonight.*

DEBBIE *reacts excitedly. She leans forward, grabs* MICHAEL's *hands.*

DEBBIE: You're *finally* going to tell them the truth?!

MICHAEL: Well. *Some* of it.

DEBBIE *abruptly drops his hands.*

DEBBIE: [*exasperated*] Michael!

MICHAEL *gestures: Don't hassle me. It's hard.*

Monique will tell them if you don't.

MICHAEL: She won't. She's too embarrassed.

DEBBIE: [*overlapping*] You're always complaining about living a lie. Here's your perfect opportunity to tell the truth.

MICHAEL: [*shaking his head*] The divorce is going to be enough of a shock... In thirty or forty years... when they've adjusted to that... I'll slip in the fact that I'm gay.

DEBBIE: You can't avoid it forever Michael—

MICHAEL: [*overlapping*] It's not as easy as you think, Debbie. If you had something this big to tell them—

DEBBIE: [*overlapping*] If I had something big to tell Mum and Dad that was sort of connected to a timeframe, and still could change, and they could affect that thing—whatever it was—then in that case I wouldn't tell them yet...

MICHAEL: [*overlapping*] What...?

DEBBIE: [*overlapping*] But if it was something they could never change, that they'd just have to learn to live with, I'd tell them.

MICHAEL: You'd tell them *tonight?*

DEBBIE: Definitely. Look, we all know Dad's got... certain faults, but do you honestly think he'd want you living a lie?

MICHAEL: Absolutely. Positively. Yes.

DEBBIE: You're right.

MICHAEL: He's a bigoted bastard.

DEBBIE: Then do it for your own peace of mind. You've been wanting to tell him for years, Michael.

MICHAEL: It's big. I have to work up to it.

DEBBIE: [*sighing*] So you keep telling me. But at this rate Dad's going to be six foot under before you find the nerve.

MICHAEL: I *will* tell him before he dies.

DEBBIE: [*sarcastic*] Fabulous. *When* before he dies?

MICHAEL: Let's not get too specific. Just before he dies, all right? I *promise* I will tell Dad I'm gay before he dies.

DEBBIE: Great. Tell him in twenty years then Michael—but don't come 'round to my place anymore moaning about you and Andrew.

> *A pretty young woman in her mid-twenties enters. This is* KAREN. *She carries a bunch of flowers and wears an engagement ring.*

KAREN: Who's Andrew?

MICHAEL/DEBBIE: Nobody. / Hi. Nobody.

KAREN: *Nobody?*

DEBBIE: Nice flowers Karen.

KAREN: This is so typical. Every time I walk into a room you two stop talking.

MICHAEL: Do you know what tonight's all about?
KAREN: That's right Michael. Change the subject.
DEBBIE: Why did we have to come over so quickly?
KAREN: You never tell *me* anything, so why should I tell you? [*Beat.*] Even if I did know.
MICHAEL: Ah. So you don't know either?
KAREN: All I know is Dad rang me and said—
MICHAEL: *Dad* rang you?

>KAREN *nods.*

When?
KAREN: Why—?
DEBBIE: *Mum* rang *us.*
MICHAEL: When did he ring you?
KAREN: I don't know... the other day—
DEBBIE: The other day?!
MICHAEL: My secretary told me. At four o'clock this afternoon.
KAREN: Well no wonder. You're always on the telephone. Poor Dad probably—(tried to get through)
MICHAEL: Poor Dad?
KAREN: Yes. Poor Dad probably tried to get through but...
DEBBIE: Karen. You are such a crawler.
KAREN: You just hate me because I'm a size eight.

>*The sound of a man clearing his throat.*

>RON *and his wife* DAWN *are entering from the bedroom area.* DAWN *is wearing her best and most sombre frock. She is very emotional. She's also tipsy—a fact which should not be immediately evident to the kids.*

RON: Michael—
MICHAEL: Dad.
RON: Debbie—
DEBBIE: Dad.
RON: *Darling.*

>KAREN *moves quickly to her father.*

KAREN: There you are, Dad...

>*She gives him a kiss and hands* DAWN *the flowers as...*

MICHAEL/DEBBIE: Why did we have to come over? / What's so important—
RON: [*interrupting*] Please, no interruptions. What I have to say is difficult enough. [*Gestures imperiously.*] Dawn.

> *She stands beside him. He pauses for effect.*

Three months ago, after suffering a series of symptoms I won't detail at this point, I sought medical advice. The news wasn't good. I was terminally ill. [*Beat.*] The long and the short of it is, I have one hundred and eight minutes left to live. Which is why you're here. I think that's all I need to say at this point.
MICHAEL/DEBBIE/KAREN: But hold on a minute— / How do you know that— / What's wrong with—
RON: [*interrupting imperiously*] Let's not make an issue out of this. The undertakers arrangements are already made so you won't need to trouble yourself with those details. Your mother's put some champagne in the fridge. I'll grab us a couple of bottles.

> RON *exits into the kitchen.* KAREN *moves to follow him as* DEBBIE *and* MICHAEL *stare at* DAWN, *aghast.*

KAREN: But... Dad... what do you mean...? You're not really dying...?

> RON *disappears into the kitchen.*

DEBBIE: Is this some kind of horrible joke?
DAWN: Your father was given three months to live at ten twenty-three pm.
MICHAEL: But that's insane!
DEBBIE: It doesn't work like that, Mum!
MICHAEL: Those timeframes are approximations! When a doctor says three months he means—
DAWN: All I know is what your father told me at lunchtime.

> *The kids look at her in shock.* KAREN *puts an arm around her.*

MICHAEL: He told you at lunchtime?

> DAWN *nods mournfully. She hiccups.*

Let me just get this completely straight: Dad told you at lunchtime today that he's going to die tonight?

> DAWN *nods again.* KAREN *strokes her arm.*

KAREN: Poor Mum. You've had to live with this all afternoon.

DAWN: He came in from the letterbox and said, 'Well Dawnie, there'll be no more gas bills for *me*'. That was when he told me he's passing away at ten twenty-three...

DEBBIE: That's ridiculous! He can't say exactly when—

DAWN: You know what your father's like Debbie. He calculates everything down to the last minute. Remember when we installed the new hot water system? Ron said it would last us nine years. And how long did it last? Nine years to the day...

DEBBIE: Mum. You can't compare a person's life to a hot water heater.

MICHAEL: This is insane. What's wrong with him? What's he got?

DAWN: Some sort of terminal illness.

MICHAEL: *Some sort* of terminal illness?!

DAWN: Michael, darling, why are you always so obsessed with detail? Your father's left a file that explains everything. We're allowed to open it at ten twenty-four.

MICHAEL: What if he doesn't die at ten twenty-three? I'm busy. I've got places to be. Are we supposed to hang around here and wait?

KAREN: Michael!

MICHAEL: Well this whole conversation is ludicrous. Dad's not going to die!

DEBBIE: Michael's right. He's perfectly healthy—

KAREN: Why are you two always so selfish? It doesn't matter whether *we* believe it. Because Dad does. And so does Mum.

DAWN: Thank you, Darling.

Turns to MICHAEL *and* DEBBIE.

And I don't think it's too much to ask for a bit of respect and consideration. These are your father's last precious moments on earth...

DEBBIE: Oh, I'm sorry Mum...

MICHAEL: I'm sorry too.

A horrible realisation hits MICHAEL.

So what we're saying, is that even though we don't necessarily believe Dad is going to die tonight, we have to behave as though he is?

DEBBIE: Exactly.

A significant look between DEBBIE *and* MICHAEL.

DAWN: We've got an hour to make Dad happy before he has to leave us forever. So let's see those smiley faces. Come on.

> DAWN *hiccups as* RON *emerges from the kitchen with two bottles of champagne.* DAWN, MICHAEL, DEBBIE *and* KAREN *turn to him with unnaturally bright smiles.*

RON: Right. Let's crack open the—(champers.)

> *Stops as he sees their 'smiles'.*

Lighten up. I'm not dead *yet.*

KAREN: Oh Dad, you're being so brave about this…

> RON *throws his arm around* KAREN*'s shoulders and squeezes her.* DAWN *watches emotionally.*

DAWN: He's the bravest man in the world.

> *She hiccups loudly.* RON *looks at her disapprovingly.*

RON: Have you been into the champers already?

DAWN: I did make a little headstart.

RON: Christ. That's all we need. Your mother dancing the can can on top of my coffin.

DAWN: I'd never do that, Ron. I can't can can.

> *Laughs at her unintended pun.*

Oh. Can't can can! That's funny, isn't it?

MICHAEL: Yeah, Mum.

RON: Here. Get that into you, Debbie.

DEBBIE: No thanks Dad. I'll stick with mineral water.

RON: You don't want to farewell your poor old father?

KAREN: Debbie—(don't be selfish.)

DAWN: It's not like you to knock back a drop, Sweetheart.

DEBBIE: I'm not feeling very well.

DAWN: Oh, you poor pumpkin.

DEBBIE: I'm fine Mum. I just—(need a quiet night.)

DAWN: You do look a bit pale.

RON: She'll survive Dawn. I just wish I could say the same for myself.

> *He sighs dramatically, coughs a little.* DEBBIE *feels guilty. She takes a glass.*

DEBBIE: I'll have one glass then.

KAREN: Just drink it and stop making such a fuss.

> RON *suddenly notices there is an extra champagne glass. He frowns, remembers something.*

RON: [*to* MICHAEL] Where's Monique?
MICHAEL: She's at her—(tai-chi class.)
DAWN: [*overriding him*] Monique's got tennis on Tuesdays.
MICHAEL: Tai-chi.
DAWN: I'm sorry, but I don't care what she calls it. I can't help feeling very hurt, Michael. I did ask especially for you both to be here.
MICHAEL: I know Mum. I'm sorry—
DEBBIE: Maybe there's another reason. Michael? Is there another reason Monique couldn't make it…?
DAWN: [*getting teary*] I think she's shown us where her priorities lie. And with your poor father about to die—
RON: Put a lid on it Dawn. I want to propose a toast.

> *He clears his throat authoritatively and raises his glass.*

To the Patterson family.
ALL: The Patterson family.

> *They clink glasses and sip their cheap champagne.* MICHAEL *spits his out.*

RON: I know I haven't always been the best father in the world—
KAREN: Yes you have!
DEBBIE: [*mimics her*] Oh yes you have!

> MICHAEL *laughs.*

KAREN: Did you see that Dad? Debbie and Michael are picking on me.
RON: Oh Sweetie…
KAREN: They do it all the time. They call me a crawler.
RON: That's bloody ridiculous.
KAREN: I'm not a crawler, am I?
RON: Of course you're not.
KAREN: Oh Dad, you're so fantastic.

> RON *glows. He gives* KAREN *a hug, oblivious to everything and everyone else.*

DAWN: [*indicating* DEBBIE *and* MICHAEL] Ron…
RON: Ah, anyway. As I was saying, running the office supplies shop

took a lot of my time and energy, especially after we opened that second branch and I pursued Mr. Matsomoto's vision for plastic points of sale... Anyway, I was very busy for a lot of years of your lives, and maybe I didn't give you enough of my time and attention. [*A little emotional.*] I hope you can all forgive me for that.

DEBBIE/MICHAEL/KAREN: Of course! / Dad... / Don't be silly.

RON: But luckily I'm a great believer in quality versus quantity. So I plan to spend the next... [*Looking at clock.*] hour and thirty-seven minutes making up for any past mistakes by giving you my undivided attention.

MICHAEL, DEBBIE *and* KAREN *are deeply touched.*

With that in mind—

RON *gets a clipboard out of the cabinet and distributes pieces of paper.*

—I've prepared a schedule of events for the evening. You'll find them colour-coded for ready reference. Please take a copy and pass them along to the person next to you.

RON *hands out copies of the schedule to his bemused family as we...*

Fade to black. The loud ticking of the clock.

Then a very neatly typed slide is projected onto the sheet on the wall. It reads: Item No. 1: A Family Prayer.

Lights up. The ticking stops.

The family now kneels in an awkward circle, hands joined. A silence. DAWN *gives* MICHAEL *a stern look.*

DAWN: Michael. We're waiting.

DAWN *hiccups.*

MICHAEL: I don't know what to say.

KAREN: Just say anything that comes into your mind.

MICHAEL: Dear...

DEBBIE: God.

MICHAEL: Thanks, Debbie. Dear God. Please bless the Saladas and sausage rolls we are about to share and bless our husband and father Ron as he prepares for—

IT'S MY PARTY (AND I'LL DIE IF I WANT TO)

MICHAEL's *mobile starts ringing from inside his suit jacket.*

Excuse me. [*Drops* DAWN's *hand, takes phone from his pocket.*] Michael Patterson. What? I told you to buy twenty-five thousand! Christ, Phil! What do you need?! An engraved invitation?! Hold on a second. [*Puts his hand over the receiver.*] This'll only take a minute. [*Back into phone.*] What? No. Of course you didn't ring at an awkward time. Get New York on the line *now* Phil! What? I don't give a flying— [*Stops himself.*] Look. I'm not interested in excuses Mate. We want twenty-five thousand yesterday! [*Etc.*]

MICHAEL *keeps talking, completely engrossed in his business conversation.*

DAWN: Maybe I should finish.

DAWN *and* DEBBIE *join hands over* MICHAEL's *head. They bow heads again.* MICHAEL *doesn't even notice.*

Dear God. Please send down your bountiful blessings on your humble but worthy son Ronald Reginald Patterson as he prepares to depart this life—

MICHAEL: [*waves distractedly*] Ssssh!

KAREN *starts crying during the final moments of* DAWN's *prayer.*

DAWN: Please grant him a safe journey into the next life and send his soul flying heavenwards like a white dove in the endless blue sky. We pray that his spirit will be soaring high above the clouds though his body may be covered by mounds of hard dirt, buried six feet below the earth in a coff—

RON: All right, all right. We get the picture. Your mother's a two pot screamer.

A giggling DAWN *sips her champagne again.*

MICHAEL: [*into phone*] Yeah. Get back to me. [*Hangs up.*] Sorry about that. Where was I? [*Grabs a couple of hands indiscriminately.*] Dear God. Please bless—

KAREN: [*interrupting disapprovingly*] We've finished Michael.

MICHAEL: Oh. Ah. [*Makes a mangled and circular Sign of the Cross.*] Amen.

Fade to black. The loud ticking of the clock.

Then another neatly typed slide is projected onto the sheet on the wall. It reads: Item No. 2: Unresolved Family Issues.

Lights up. The loud ticking stops.

The family is now sitting at the table which is positioned lengthways away from the audience. RON *sits facing the audience. The clock is on the wall directly behind him.* MICHAEL *and* DEBBIE *sit on one side,* DAWN *and* KAREN *on the other.* KAREN *is a little tense after her Private Moments.*

RON: What I'd like to do now is discuss with you kids as a group how you feel I've managed as a father. If you've got any queries or unresolved issues, I'd like to hear them. Any gripes you have with me at all.

DEBBIE and MICHAEL are filled with fire. At last, here's the chance to vent their spleens.

DEBBIE/MICHAEL: Well, since you're asking— / As a matter of fact, I—
RON: [*interrupting*] You know, you do your best to put a roof over your kids' heads, sacrifice your dreams for theirs, and try and save enough of yourself to be there when they've got a problem. And then suddenly one day you're staring death in the face, and you have to wonder if that was enough. Who knows? Anyway. You were saying?

The kids recognise this emotional blackmail for what it is, but it works regardless. Their backdown is grudging.

DEBBIE/MICHAEL: Nothing.
RON: You were going to say something.

KAREN *gives* DEBBIE *and* MICHAEL *a look: don't you dare.*

DEBBIE/MICHAEL: No we weren't. / No complaints Dad.
RON: *No* complaints? Guess I'm not such a bad bloke after all…

RON's *thrilled he got out of this so easily. But* DAWN *wants to get things out in the open, for everybody's sake.*

DAWN: Ron I think there probably are some—(complaints.)
RON: [*interrupting briskly*] Right. Let's move straight onto the next item then! Private Moments with Michael.
MICHAEL: [*panics*] Ah. How long are these Private Moments going to be?

RON: Time's not exactly on our side, but they'll be long enough to resolve any long-term hostility and reach a greater depth of understanding for each other. Around four to five minutes, depending.

MICHAEL: Depending on what?

RON: On if we run overtime on other scheduled events.

MICHAEL *anxiously peruses his copy of the agenda.*

MICHAEL: Let me just get something straight. Debbie's Private Moments are up second last. So if everything else takes longer than expected, does that mean you might not talk to her alone?

RON: I'm hoping that she won't miss out, but yes, that may be the case.

MICHAEL: Can I swap my Private Moments with yours?

DAWN: Now Michael. Your father made the schedule the way he thinks best. And I think we should respect his wishes, don't you?

MICHAEL: Yes Mum.

MICHAEL *smiles weakly at* DEBBIE. *She grimaces. Good luck!*

Fade to black. The loud ticking of the clock.

Another neatly typed slide is projected onto the sheet on the wall. It reads: Item No. 3: Private Moments–Michael.

Lights up. The loud ticking stops.

MICHAEL *and* RON *are now alone in the living room.* MICHAEL *smiles awkwardly.* RON *makes a gesture: follow me. He leads the way to the sideboard and picks up a trophy.*

RON: You know how proud I was when you won this?

MICHAEL: That's a netball trophy. [*Points.*] I won the spoon. Most Consistent at soccer.

RON: [*picks up a tiny teaspoon*] Of course you did. And I felt as if my heart was going to burst that day. But I have to tell you Michael, that's nothing compared to the pride I feel right now.

MICHAEL: Dad—

RON: [*interrupting*] The father/son bond is a very special thing. We're the same man, a generation apart. But while we're the same we're very different too. Would you agree with that?

MICHAEL: Definitely. And that's why—

RON: [*interrupting*] So tell me about yourself Mate. Tell me about Michael Patterson the man. I want to know what makes you tick.

MICHAEL: I'm glad you feel that way Dad, because there *is* something I want to tell you. This is... it's really important to me. And I feel—very strongly—that I should take this opportunity to be completely honest with you...

RON: I'm all ears Mate.

MICHAEL *clears his throat nervously.*

MICHAEL: Hhhmmm... the thing is Dad, what I'm about to tell you might come as a... well, it might not—no, it *will definitely* come as a shock to you. And...

RON: I don't think there's much that can surprise a man of my age.

MICHAEL: You'd be surprised.

MICHAEL *pauses, trying to find the courage and the words. A long silence.* RON *fidgets a little.*

RON: Come on. What's on your mind Mate? Get it off your chest.

MICHAEL: Well. It's... ah... it's about me and Monique...

RON *nudges* MICHAEL *in a matey fashion.*

RON: She's bloody beautiful, Son!

MICHAEL: Yeah Dad, she is, but in spite of that...

RON: You don't have to say another word. Your mother might get stroppy with Monique now and then, but she was your choice, and *I* respect that.

MICHAEL: And I appreciate you respecting that—but what I'm trying to say is that... ah... Monique can't give me everything I... the thing is... ah, sexually...

RON: [*winks*] I know what you're saying Son. When I see a pair of beautiful tits walk past! [*Shaking his head.*] There's a lot of temptations.

MICHAEL: There are other temptations too Dad. And that's what I'd like to talk about—(now.)

RON: Kids'll fix it.

MICHAEL: What?

RON: You and Monique need to start a family. That'll get your mind off the skirts. Your mother'd love to be a grandma too. It'd give her something to focus on after I'm—(gone.)

MICHAEL: Dad. Listen to me. Just for a second. [*Beat.*] I'm attracted to people who resemble myself.

RON: You've got a healthy ego. That's no crime.
MICHAEL: No. What I mean is—

> MICHAEL's *mobile phone starts ringing.*

Damn. Excuse me. [*Picks up phone.*] Michael Patterson. Yeah Phil. What did New York say? Yeah? Well tell 'em they can get fu—ah, forget that! Get onto Bill Sedgewick. Now! Get back to me!

> MICHAEL *hangs up.* RON *smiles proudly.*

RON: That's the way Son. If you're making friends, you're not making money.
MICHAEL: Dad. Please… just listen while I tell you about me and Monique…
RON: There's more?
MICHAEL: There's a lot more. It's… we're…

> MICHAEL *pauses again.* RON *is getting impatient. He looks over his shoulder at the clock.*

RON: You'll have to make it snappy if we want to stay on schedule.
MICHAEL: Well I recently told her I'm… (gay) and so we decided to… (separate) and now she's… (moving out)
RON: You sly bugger! She's already pregnant!

> MICHAEL *can't be bothered arguing. He smiles miserably as* RON *enthusiastically shakes his hand.*

Congratulations!
MICHAEL: Thanks Dad.

> *Fade to black. The loud ticking of the clock.*

> *Another neatly typed slide is projected onto the sheet on the wall. This slide reads:* Item No. 4: Discussion of Upcoming Family Events Ron Won't Be Attending For Obvious Reasons.

> *Lights up. The loud ticking stops.*

> *The entire family is once again gathered in the living room.* DEBBIE *is trying to catch* MICHAEL's *eye, but he won't look at her.* RON *is irritated by not having* DEBBIE's *attention. From now on* MICHAEL's *tension is far more overt.*

RON: Deb…? Deb…? Deborah. Front and centre, thank you. [*Pats the chair beside him.*] Dawn.

> DEBBIE *is forced to sit down.* RON *ticks off the prayer and the Private Moments with Michael on his clipboard.*

Item Number Four—Discussion of Upcoming Family Events that Ron—ie. me—won't be attending... for obvious reasons.

> KAREN *sniffles sadly. But* RON *is still quite excited by what he's just 'learned'.*

I think we should start this item with some news from Michael and Monique.

DEBBIE: [*to* MICHAEL] You *did* tell him?

> RON *winks at* MICHAEL. MICHAEL *sits in sullen silence.*

RON: He did. And I'm proud of him.
DEBBIE: Ffff—God!!
KAREN: What did he tell you?
RON: Michael? Why don't you share it with your mother and sisters?
DAWN: What is it Sweetheart?
DEBBIE: I've got to say Dad, I'm stunned. You're taking this incredibly well.
RON: It was a bolt from the blue, I admit, but—
KAREN: What is it Michael?
DAWN: Tell us Darling!
RON: Come on Mate. Spill the beans.
MICHAEL: Well... it's... ah...
RON: Oh, stop fartarsing around Son. Michael and Monique are having a baby!
DAWN: Oh Michael, Sweetheart! I'm going to be a grandma!
KAREN: That's fantastic, Michael. Congratulations!
DEBBIE: [*amused*] Yeah. Congratulations.
KAREN: [*to* DEBBIE] How come he told you but he didn't tell me?
DAWN: Oh, I've always loved Monique! How many weeks is she? Michael? Darling?
RON: Now I don't want you on Michael's back, Dawn. He's chosen to keep it a secret this long—
KAREN: He told Debbie.
RON: I'm sure he had his reasons for that. But when it comes to the crunch this is a private matter between Michael and Monique. [*Winks.*] Isn't that right, Son?
MICHAEL: Let's talk about other upcoming events. There must be

something more important than this.

DAWN: What's more important than our very first grandchild?

RON: A brand new Patterson! Let's drink to the little bloke, eh?

KAREN: Doesn't anyone care about my wedding? I thought *that* was an important upcoming event.

MICHAEL: Yeah Dad! Let's talk about Karen's wedding!

KAREN: You don't have to if you're not interested.

RON: Of course I'm interested! I want to hear all about it. What are you wearing?

KAREN: Ivory silk taffeta with a sweetheart neckline and leg-o-mutton sleeves.

DAWN: And Craig and his groomsmen are wearing green bow ties and cummerbunds.

KAREN: Mum I told you I don't like cummerbunds.

DAWN: But they look so smart, Karen.

KAREN: No they don't. They look daggy.

DAWN: Well I don't think so. But what would I know? I'm only the bride's mother.

KAREN: Debbie. Don't cummerbunds look dumb?

DEBBIE: They *can*, yeah. But not always. Sometimes—

KAREN: Oh forget it. Why am I asking *you?* She won't even be my bridesmaid.

RON: Why not?

DEBBIE: Karen, you know I'd love to stand beside you on your wedding day. But you're having apricot taffeta with ruffles. I'm thirty-two years old. I can't wear apricot taffeta with ruffles. I'd look like one of those dolls on top of a toilet roll.

DAWN: I think you'd look lovely.

DEBBIE: You know I'll do anything else to make the day special for you, but—

KAREN: I'm sorry *you* haven't found a husband. All right.

DEBBIE: What?

KAREN: I'm sorry you're eight years older than me and you still haven't found someone to marry you. But I don't see why you should take it out on me.

DEBBIE: Oh, grow up Karen!

KAREN: Well you're jealous, aren't you? I'm not saying I blame you. I would be too if I was you. But I don't see why that means you can't co-operate with my wedding.

RON: Your little sister's got a good point Debbie. We all feel for you in your situation, but you have to be big enough not to let your jealousy spoil the best day of Karen's life.

DEBBIE: I am *not* jealous! I'm very happy for Karen! [*Beat.*] Mu-u-u-u-m!

DAWN: I know you're happy for your sister Debbie, but I think being a bridesmaid would be a nice way to show it.

DEBBIE *takes a few deep breaths, tries to calm down.*

DEBBIE: Look. I'd rather not get tense or agitated right now. So could we please talk about something else?

KAREN: All right. Whatever you say. Let's just pretend my wedding's not even happening.

DEBBIE: Oh, please. [*Sighs.*] Look. Michael… help me out here.

MICHAEL: [*terse*] She doesn't want to be a bridesmaid because she'll look stupid in the dress.

RON: Maybe if she wore dresses a bit more often she wouldn't be alone in the first place. [*Beat.*] Men like to see a girl in a dress. There's nothing more sexy than sneaking a peak at a pretty ankle. Isn't that right Michael?

MICHAEL *grunts non-committally.*

You never know. You might even meet a nice bloke at the wedding.

DAWN: Now there's a thought. Karen, are there any nice single men coming for Debbie?

KAREN: I don't think I know any old enough.

DEBBIE: Look. I appreciate everybody's concern, really. But I'm fine. I've got a great life. I've got a wonderful job, lots of loyal friends, a… [*Can't think of a complimentary adjective.*] family. I can afford to go places and pursue my interests. I'm blessed. And I just happen to be single. So what?

RON: [*sighs*] I just worry about you growing old alone.

DEBBIE: I'm not going to grow old alone.

KAREN: That's right Dad. She'll have my children to play with.

RON: That's a thoughtful offer Sweetie. Debbie, you should take your little sister up on that.

DEBBIE: [*through gritted teeth*] I will.

RON: Good. You'll make a wonderful aunty one day. [*Beat.*] And in the meantime I think you should get yourself a cat.
DEBBIE: Could we *please* get back to the cummerbunds?
DAWN: Oh. Well I think they're lovely but—
RON: Dawn. Your day's long gone Woman. Karen knows better.
KAREN: Mum's got a right to an opinion Dad. If she likes them—
DAWN: But you *don't* Sweetheart—
KAREN: But if you do—
DAWN: But it's your day Karen. And if you feel that strongly—
KAREN: But you feel strongly too—
RON: [*interrupting*] This whole thing's shaping up to be a bloody bunfight. I'm glad I won't be around for it!
DAWN: Ron!
RON: I'm sorry Sweetie. I suppose I'm just letting off some steam, because it breaks my heart to think of you walking up that aisle without me.
KAREN: [*a thought occuring*] Dad. If I can't walk up the aisle with you, I think… in spite of the cummerbund situation… I'd like *Mum* to give me away.
DEBBIE: I think that's a great idea.
DAWN: Oh, Karen!
RON: Your *mother?*
KAREN: If Michael doesn't mind.
MICHAEL: Absolutely not.
KAREN: Mum?
DAWN: Oh Sweetheart. I'd be the proudest woman in the world.
RON: I like this idea as much as anyone, but I have to ask whether it's appropriate.
DAWN/DEBBIE/MICHAEL/KAREN: What do you mean? / Why not? / What's wrong with it? [*Etc.*]
RON: I've never seen a mother do it before.
KAREN: So? Just because you haven't seen it before…
RON: Have you Dawn? Ever seen it?
DAWN: Well no Ron, but… [*Voice trails off.*]
RON: Much as I like the idea, it's a man's job. Michael should give Karen away.
MICHAEL: Karen wants Mum to do it.
DAWN: Do you really think it's inappropriate, Ron?

DEBBIE: Of course it's not inappropriate.

RON: [*to* DAWN] You'll be busy with flowers and what-not won't you?

KAREN: Dad why are you trying to spoil it for Mum? She wants to do it. And *I* want her to, too.

RON: And you'll have your hostessing duties don't forget.

MICHAEL: Are you deaf as well as terminally diseased? Karen wants *Mum* to give her away!

DAWN: Michael! How can you talk to your poor father like that? The man's got an hour to live!

MICHAEL: I'm sorry Mum, but I'm sick to death of the way he tries to manipulate—(things his way)

RON: It's all right Son. You don't have to explain. Anger is one of the five stages of grief. He seems to be making an early start.

DAWN: Oh Sweetheart, I should have realised...

KAREN: So it's settled then. Mum's going to give me away. [*Beat.*] It is settled. Isn't it? Dad?

    RON *gives a little wheeze for effect.*

RON: Apparently.

DAWN: Oh Ron... I wish you could be there to see it.

RON: Why can't I see it now? [*Beat.*] Let's have a trial run for your old Dad. So I can picture it, and pack it away in my mind to take up to... [*Waves his hand vaguely in the air.*] wherever I'm going, with me.

DAWN: Karen, Sweetheart?

KAREN: I don't think you'll get much of an idea.

RON: Any idea is better than nothing.

KAREN: I don't want to Dad. Craig isn't here and I haven't got my dress and the bridesmaids aren't here and—

    RON *starts coughing.* KAREN *feels instantly obliged.*

Are you all right? All right... I'll do it.

    RON *instantly 'recovers'. He briskly takes control, moving furniture to form a makeshift aisle.*

RON: Right. I'll make an aisle. [*To* KAREN.] You go and pop your face on. [*Moving furniture.*] Debbie. Make yourself useful. Michael, give me a hand Mate.

    The slightest hint of hesitation from the increasingly disgruntled MICHAEL *and...*

Come on. On your bike, Mike.

MICHAEL *grumpily helps* RON *as* DAWN *grabs* KAREN*'s arm.*

DAWN: Debbie. Can you get the lace tablecloth out of the linen cupboard Sweetheart. I'd get it myself but I'm not sure I can walk that far.

She giggles in a tipsy manner. RON *rolls his eyes.* KAREN *is getting a little tetchy.*

RON: Christ Dawn. You're a bloody embarrassment.

KAREN: She's just having a good time, Dad.

DAWN: We're *all* having a good time, aren't we Sweetheart?

KAREN *is holding* DAWN *up. She almost trips.* RON *grunts disparagingly.* DEBBIE *brings the lace tablecloth over.*

DEBBIE: What do you want this for?

DAWN: I'm going to put it on Karen's head.

KAREN: What…? Mum…

DAWN: [*overlapping*] Come on Sweetheart. Quick sticks.

DAWN *puts the lace tablecloth on* KAREN*'s head.* KAREN *is getting more irritated every second.* DEBBIE*'s laughing.*

Oh, lovely… Ron, look! She looks like an angel.

KAREN *frowns as her eye catches something on the edge of the lace tablecloth.*

KAREN: What's that?

DAWN: A pickle stain.

DAWN *giggles drunkenly.*

KAREN: [*agitated*] Can we start now, please?

RON: I'm the minister. Michael, you're the congregation.

He gestures impatiently for the morose MICHAEL *to stand up.* MICHAEL *ignores him.*

DEBBIE: What about me?

RON: You're the bridesmaid.

DEBBIE: Dad weren't you listening to anything before? I'm not going to be—(a bridesmaid.)

RON *coughs and wheezes some more.*

DAWN: Ron? Are you all right?

RON: I just wish people would be a bit more helpful…
KAREN: Don't worry about Debbie. She hates me. I'm used to it.
DEBBIE: I do not hate you.
KAREN: You do so. [*To* RON.] She hates me!
RON: [*wheezing, to* DEBBIE] Are you happy now your sour grapes have ruined the best day of your sister's life?

> DEBBIE *almost loses her temper.*

DEBBIE: I *do not have sour*— [*Stops, controls herself.*] All right, all right. If it means that much to everybody… I'll do it.
DAWN: Good girl. [*Pointing*] Use those flowers as your bouquet Sweetheart.

> DEBBIE *takes the flowers that* KAREN *brought* DAWN *earlier in the evening and holds them as a bouquet, complete with vase.*

DEBBIE: Can we just get this over with?
KAREN: Let's just do it. Please?
DAWN: I think I'm going to cry!
RON: All rise.

> MICHAEL *ignores him.* RON *gets a little impatient.*

Congregation rise.

> MICHAEL *grumpily gets to his feet.*

I'll hum the music. Michael, you help. One-two-three—Da da da da! Da da da—

> MICHAEL *hums with a decided lack of enthusiasm.* DAWN *and* KAREN *start walking behind* DEBBIE. KAREN *is basically propping* DAWN *up.*

KAREN: Debbie! You're walking too fast!
DEBBIE: Sorry.

> DEBBIE *slows down dramatically.*

RON: Dawn! Stand up straight, Woman!
DAWN: I don't think I can.
DEBBIE: Is this slow—(enough?)
KAREN: [*interrupting*] Mum! Watch out!

> *But too late.* KAREN *and* DAWN *run up the back of* DEBBIE. *They all fall over.*

DAWN: [*giggles*] Ooops. We ran up Debbie's bottom.
DEBBIE: [*overlapping*] Are you okay, Mum?
KAREN: [*overlapping*] When I said slow down I didn't mean stop.
DEBBIE: I didn't stop.
MICHAEL: [*picking* DAWN *up*] Mum… are you all right?
DAWN: [*overlapping*] I feel all wobbly.
RON: No bloody wonder. Sit down and stay out of mischief. Michael. You're taking over.
MICHAEL: No I'm not.

> RON *starts coughing and wheezing again.*

RON: I want to see you walk your sister up the aisle.
MICHAEL: Karen wants *Mum* to walk her up the aisle.

> *Beat as* RON *wheezes with conviction.*

Are you okay?
DAWN: Ron? Are you all right Darling?
KAREN: You should rest, Dad. And I don't like doing this anyway.
RON: [*coughing and wheezing*] I'd just love to see you all… one last time…

> RON*'s voice trails off as though he is too weak to speak further. They gather around him anxiously.*

MICHAEL: [*weakening*] Dad. Karen wants Mum to give her away.
KAREN: I don't want anyone to. Not today. I feel like we're making a mockery.
RON: [*wheezing, to* MICHAEL] Please? Can't I see you giving your sister away and Debbie being bridesmaid?
DEBBIE: I don't want to…

> RON *wheezes and doubles over as though in intense pain.* DAWN *rushes to his side.*

DAWN: [*wobbly legs*] Ron! Darling! Are you all right?
RON: [*overlapping, coughing*] Is it too much for a dying man to ask?

> DEBBIE *and* MICHAEL *know that* RON *is manipulating them. But at the same time his wheezes are making them anxious. They exchange a look, intercepted by* KAREN.

KAREN: If you won't even do it when Dad's this sick—!
MICHAEL: You said *you* don't want to do it!

KAREN: I don't.
DEBBIE: Then Karen—
KAREN: [*interrupting*] But Dad wants to see it! And he's practically dead!

> RON *wheezes loudly. Coughs for additional impact.*

DAWN: Ron, darling! Please Michael, Debbie?
MICHAEL: Okay. Of course.
DEBBIE: I'm sorry. We'll do it.

> *Instantly* RON's *coughs and wheezes cease. He stands up straight. He takes control.*

RON: Michael. Take your sister's arm—

> RON *grabs* MICHAEL's *arm and arranges it around* KAREN's *arm.* MICHAEL *shrugs him off in irritation.*

MICHAEL: I know what to do, Dad.
RON: Debbie, you walk about two and half feet in front.
KAREN: Is it that horrible to hold my hand for two seconds?
MICHAEL: Oh, what?
KAREN: You yanked your arm away like I smell or something!
MICHAEL: Karen—
DEBBIE: [*overlapping*] Can we just get this over with please?
KAREN: That's your whole attitude to my wedding, isn't it?
DEBBIE: *You're* the one who's been saying—(you didn't want to do this)
RON: [*interrupting*] For Christ's sake leave your little sister alone!
DEBBIE: What did I say?
RON: [*interrupting*] I'm fed up with you two picking on poor Karen.
MICHAEL: *Me?* What did *I* do?
RON: [*yells*] You get down the other end of the room and give your bloody sister away!

> KAREN *furiously pulls the tablecloth off her head. She bursts into tears.*

KAREN: [*crying*] I don't want to do it anymore! I've got to get this tablecloth off—my—head! I just want to stop! All right?!

> RON *makes his way over to* KAREN. *He puts his arms around her and fixes a furious glare on* DEBBIE *and* MICHAEL.

RON: It's okay Sweetie, you don't have to do it. [*To* MICHAEL *and* DEBBIE.] I hope you two are pleased with yourselves.

Fade to black. The loud ticking of the clock.

Another neatly typed slide is projected onto the sheet on the wall. It reads: Item No. 5: Family Slides (In No Particular Order).

The loud ticking stops but the lights remain off and the slide is replaced by Slide #1 that shows a smiling group of young parents and infant children around a Christmas tree.

RON now stands behind the slide projector. DEBBIE, DAWN, MICHAEL *and* KAREN *are seated on chairs arranged in rows. The air is thick with tension.* KAREN *is openly crying.*

DEBBIE: What year was that?

Almost before her question is finished, RON *has ripped the slide off.*

DAWN: 1974, when you were—(four)

RON whips the slide away.

Ron?

RON: Time's working against us. The wedding practice took longer than it would have if people had been more co-operative.

RON puts Slide #2 up. It's a group of people at a christening in the early seventies. Ad-lib sighs, reactions.

That was... ah... someone's christening.

DAWN: [*full of emotion*] It was Debbie's.

DEBBIE: Mine? Which baby am I?

MICHAEL: [*grins*] The fat one.

DAWN: [*overlapping*] You're the one in the middle, Sweetheart, see? And there's Michael standing next to Aunty Lorraine.

DEBBIE gets to her feet and moves closer to the slide to get a better look. She looks like a shadow puppet.

DEBBIE: *Which* baby am I? [*Points.*] This—(one?)

RON whips the slide away as DEBBIE stands looking at it.

RON: We've got a lot of slides to get through. Sit down.

>   RON *moves to Slide #3. It shows three happy young couples gathered around a Christmas tree. The reminiscence surrounding this slide is strictly between* RON *and* DAWN.

DAWN: Ah, there's the old gang...
RON: That would've been at Christmas drinks.
DAWN: [*overlapping*] Oh, remember those Christmases Ron? We used to find mistletoe *everywhere!*
KAREN: [*sniffles sulkily*] How come *I'm* never in the family slides?

>   RON *moves to Slide #4. It shows a woman and a group of kids sitting beside a snowman.*

RON: Here you are Sweetie.
DAWN: With Mr Snowman.
KAREN: I remember that Snowman! We made him with the Johnsons. But *I* put his buttons on didn't I?
RON: [*overlapping*] That's right Sweetie. I showed you how.
MICHAEL: No you didn't.
RON: Yes I did. And then I showed her how to make his hat.
MICHAEL: Me and Debbie made that snowman's hat.
RON: No. *I* showed Karen how to sculpt the snow and then—
MICHAEL: [*interrupting belligerently*] Debbie didn't *we* make that snowman's hat?
DEBBIE: Yeah. Me and Michael made the hat.
MICHAEL: See Dad? You're wrong!
RON: I paid for every one of those bloody holidays. I ought to know what went on.
MICHAEL: Yeah, well that was the winter I was in Year Eight. And you weren't even there yet!
RON: [*doesn't believe him*] I wasn't there? Then who took the photo?
DAWN: Uncle Barry did.

>   RON *stops and stares at* DAWN *disparagingly.*

Umm... you *were* a bit late for that holiday Ron. You hadn't actually arrived yet.
MICHAEL: See?!
RON: So *you* made the snowman's bloody hat. Let's not make an issue out of it.

>   RON *moves between slides of the family on holidays with cousins*

and other relatives. He moves through them faster and faster as he looks towards the clock.

Slide #5.

DEBBIE: Oh look. There's Cousin Louise. Is she still living in Wagga Wagga?

DAWN: Oh yes. Three children now.

RON: *Three* kids. And she's only twenty-eight. Her parents are very proud.

Slide #6.

KAREN: Whose party was that?

DAWN: It was Michael's sixth birthday. Look Michael, there's Sally Smithkin in the little pink hat.

KAREN: [*peers at the slide*] Oh, she was cute…

RON: Sally was a good girl. Quiet and respectful. Michael could have had her if he wanted her.

MICHAEL: Dad.

KAREN: What's so great about being quiet and respectful?

RON: [*overlapping*] She had her eye on your big brother the whole time they were growing up. But Michael was too busy with all his other birds. Eh, Mate?

MICHAEL *grunts non-committally.*

She married another fella in the end. She was one girl who had no shortage of offers.

DEBBIE: [*a little touchy*] What's that supposed to mean?

RON: Nothing.

Slide #7.

DAWN: Oh, there you all are outside the tent—

Slide #8.

MICHAEL: And there's that canoe Cousin Jamie had. We pushed him out of it once and—(he fell into the water)

Slide #9.

DEBBIE: Oh. I remember that teddy bear. It was my favourite. I used to—(take it everywhere)

Slide #10.

DAWN: There's me and Dad on the toboggan! We beat—(Lorraine and Barry every race)

Slide #11.

KAREN: Could you slow down a bit Dad?

RON: We're way behind schedule.

KAREN: But—

Slide #12, Slide #13, Slide #14, Slide #15, Slide #16. Slide #14 shows a boy of about sixteen proudly holding up a fish.

DEBBIE: Stop for a second! Go back! Go back!

RON *goes back to Slide #14.*

Peter Jenkins. I'd forgotten all about him.

DAWN: Your first boyfriend ever. He was lovely.

MICHAEL: He was a loser.

RON: He'd be married with kids now.

DEBBIE: Like everyone except *me*, you mean. [*Beat.*] That's what you mean, isn't it?

RON: What are you being so touchy about?

DEBBIE: I'm not being touchy.

RON: You're doing a bloody good impression of it.

DEBBIE: Well Dad, have you ever stopped to listen to yourself? You define everyone by their marital status.

RON: Can I help it if everyone else is married?

DEBBIE: See? That's it. That's your attitude. It's like being single makes me a social outcast.

RON: [*sighs patronisingly*] The only person who makes an issue out of you not having a man is you.

DEBBIE: Bullshit!

DAWN: Debbie!

DEBBIE: I'm fine when I'm away from here—I couldn't care less—but as soon as I walk in the front door I feel this huge *pressure*—(coming down on me)

RON: [*interrupting*] That's all in your head.

DEBBIE: How can you say that? Whenever—(I come home...)

RON: [*interrupting*] Well what's so bloody hard about it for Christ's sake? You go out, you meet a man, you go to the movies, you get engaged. Everyone else can do it.

DEBBIE *can't stand it any longer. She jumps to her feet and stands in front of the projector. She looks like a particularly aggressive shadow puppet.*

DEBBIE: [*interrupting, screaming*] It's your fault I'm still single!

Advances towards him.

It's *your* fault I always pick the wrong men!

DAWN *stands up, another shadow puppet.*

DAWN: *Our* fault?!

DEBBIE: No! *His* fault!

RON: Why is it *my* fault?!

DEBBIE: Because you've always been... you're so... you're... *emotionally unavailable!*

RON: Emotionally what—?

DEBBIE: And now I end up with emotionally unavailable men!

DAWN: Now Debbie, I don't think this is the time—

DEBBIE: I'm always trying to win their attention. Just like I'm always trying to win yours. And when I win it, it isn't worth it!

DAWN: Deborah—

DEBBIE: I've watched Oprah, Mum. I know how it works!

KAREN: For God's sake Debbie. Don't you think this belongs in your Private Moments?

RON: It's all right Sweetie. She's obviously quite upset. We can deviate from the agenda. Briefly.

DEBBIE: See?! See?!

RON: What? What?

DEBBIE: It's going to kill you to "deviate from the agenda" to discuss something that means this much to me! I'm not Item Number Nine. I'm your *daughter!*

RON: Could we just tone down the hysteria a little—

DEBBIE: When we were kids you were always pre-occupied. Your mind was on stationery supplies or some other stupid thing. I remember when I was little, and I'd do a forward roll. I'd say, 'Look Mum, look Dad. I can do a forward roll!' And Mum would always look. From the start to the finish. But you only pretended. Because when I put my head up again you'd be looking somewhere else. And you'd turn back and say, 'That's was great Debbie! Clever girl!' But you hadn't even been looking.

RON: So that's what this is all about? Because I didn't watch you do a somersault?
DEBBIE: Oh, what's the point?
MICHAEL: For once in your selfish life Dad. Stop thinking about yourself for thirty seconds and *listen* to what Debbie's telling you.
DAWN: Michael!
RON: Well, all right then… do one now.
DEBBIE: What?
RON: Do a forward roll now.

> RON *moves over and turns the light back on.*

Come on. Do a somersault for me.

> DEBBIE *looks non-plussed, to say the least.*

You've got my undivided attention.
DAWN: That's a nice idea Sweetheart. Do a forward roll for Dad.
DEBBIE: I can't do a forward roll now.
DAWN: Of course you can.
RON: I'm waiting.
DAWN: Go on Debbie. Your father's watching.
DEBBIE: Mum I don't feel well. Remember?
RON: One small somersault won't hurt you.
DAWN: It'll be over in thirty seconds Sweetheart, and think how happy you'll be that Dad was watching!
RON: You'll have my complete concentration.
DEBBIE: What's the point in me doing a somersault here? That's not the issue.
RON: I thought that was exactly the issue.
DAWN: Your father's trying to meet you halfway Darling.

> DAWN *hiccups.* DEBBIE *looks helplessly to* MICHAEL *and* KAREN.

KAREN: [*impatient*] You're always saying Dad never pays attention.
DEBBIE: But this isn't going to—(change anything)
KAREN: [*interrupting*] He's paying attention. What else do you want?
DAWN: Come on Sweetheart. Time's against us.
MICHAEL: Just do it and get it over with.
DEBBIE: Michael!
DAWN: Come on Debbie.
RON: I'm waiting.

MICHAEL: [*overlapping*] They won't get off your back 'til you do.
RON: I am not on Debbie's back. I'm simply demonstrating my interest in watching her do a forward roll.
DEBBIE: This is ridiculous...
DAWN: [*overlapping*] Come on Sweetheart.
KAREN: [*overlapping*] What's the problem *now?*
MICHAEL: [*overlapping*] Just do it.
RON: Tell you what—why don't I do a forward roll too? And you don't even have to watch me do mine.
DEBBIE: No Dad. It's... all right. I'll do it.
DAWN: Good girl.

> DEBBIE *sighs and prepares for the feat.*

DEBBIE: I can't believe I'm doing this.
DAWN: We're all watching Debbie.
RON: Especially me.

> RON *leans forward intently, self-consciously focusing all his attention on* DEBBIE. DEBBIE *bends herself at the knees, preparing...*

DAWN: Good luck.
KAREN: [*overlapping*] Hurry up.

> As DEBBIE *starts to lean over she notices* RON *glancing furtively at the clock.*

DEBBIE: Here goes... He's looking at the clock!
RON: I am not.
DAWN: Come on Sweetheart. Just do it.
MICHAEL: Go, Deb.

> DEBBIE *angrily throws her dignified thirty-two year old body into an undignified somersault on the floor. Halfway through she twists her back.*

DEBBIE: Oww!
RON: What's wrong?
DEBBIE: [*hunched over*] Oww!

> *Everyone rushes to help* DEBBIE. RON *and* DAWN *get there first. They help her up, physically supporting her. She's hunched over in pain.*

DAWN: What happened?

DEBBIE: [*grumpy*] My back!
RON: That was a terrific forward roll Sweetie. Spot-on.
DEBBIE: Shut-up!!!!

She stamps her foot, then squeals in pain. It hurt her back.

DAWN: Debbie!
RON: What have I done now?
DEBBIE: It's your fault! Everything's your fault!
RON: *Everything's* my fault?
DEBBIE: Yes!
RON: Well, thank Christ for that. Now we know why the world's going wrong. It's *my* fault the Yanks pissed off Osama bin Laden, it's *my* fault Warnie did his shoulder, it's *my* fault you're still single.
DEBBIE: Yes! Yes! Yes!
RON: Far be it from me to bring some icy cold logic to this, but Michael and Karen had the same father as you. And Karen's getting married.
DEBBIE: Really? Nobody mentioned that.
KAREN: She *has* to be mean to me, Dad. She hates me.
DAWN: Now Debbie, it's not Karen's fault.
DEBBIE: Well I'm not Karen and she's not me—
KAREN: [*overlapping*] Thank goodness!
DEBBIE: [*overlapping*] Besides, by the time Karen came along you were more interested.
RON: But what about Michael? He was born before you were, and he found Monique.
MICHAEL: Monique and me aren't a good example to use—
RON: Of course you are. That girl worships the ground you walk on. You've been married nine years—
MICHAEL: [*overlapping*] She hates me Dad. We're getting a divorce.
DAWN: What?!
MICHAEL: There. I said it. We're getting a divorce.
KAREN: You're getting divorced?!
RON: Why didn't you tell us?
MICHAEL: It's a mutual thing.
DAWN: Oh Michael—what's happened Darling? Has she met someone else?
MICHAEL: No Mum. *I've* met someone else.
RON: *You've* met someone else?

MICHAEL *nods.*

KAREN: You're leaving Monique for someone else?

MICHAEL *nods again.*

RON: Well. Who is she?

MICHAEL *is silent.*

DAWN: Who's this girl who's stolen your heart?
RON: Come on Son. What's her name?

The briefest hesitation before MICHAEL *says...*

MICHAEL: Andrew.

A long silence.

DAWN: Did you say... *Andrea?*
MICHAEL: No Mum. I said Andrew. [*Beat.*] I'm gay.

A long silence as RON, DAWN *and* KAREN *stare at him. Then...*

RON: [*incredulous*] He's a bloody poofter.
DAWN: But you're married. To a girl. With blonde hair and eyeshadow...
MICHAEL: I know this is a huge thing to dump on you all. I don't expect you to assimilate it straight—(away)
KAREN: [*interrupting, wrinkled nose*] Oh my God, this is so revolting. You actually... *do things* with *other men?!*
MICHAEL: I'm intimate with one man, Karen.
RON: For Christ's sake, spare us the details!
DAWN: But I don't understand... How can you just suddenly become a... [*She pauses, the word is difficult to say.*] ... homosexual?
MICHAEL: There's nothing sudden about it Mum. I've known I was gay since I was sixteen.
RON: I should never have sent you on that Sea Scouts Bivouac!
DEBBIE: That's an intelligent reaction Dad.
KAREN: How come you're so calm? He told you, didn't he? Why didn't you tell me?
MICHAEL: Mum, I'm sorry. I know this is a horrible shock...
DAWN: It's our fault. It must be our fault. Was there too much classical music in the house?
MICHAEL: It's not your fault Mum. It's just a fact. And that fact's got nothing to do with you or Dad.
RON: You're bloody right it doesn't.

MICHAEL *makes a move towards his father.* RON *backs away ever so slightly.*

MICHAEL: Dad. I knew this would horrify you. That's why I've never told you before. Well, I tried to tell you in my Private Moments, but as usual you wouldn't shut up for long enough to—anyway, that's… the thing is… I know that even if you live to be—well, [*Looks at clock.*] fifty minutes older, you'll probably still never understand. But can't you at least respect me for my honesty?

RON *looks like he's going to do just that. He picks up a champagne glass.*

RON: I think I need some more champagne.

He lifts it towards his lips, then suddenly stops.

You haven't drunk out of this, have you?

MICHAEL: [*lunges for him*] You bastard!

DEBBIE, DAWN *and* KAREN *race forward to stop him.*

DAWN/DEBBIE/KAREN: Michael! / Stop! / Don't! [*Etc.*]

MICHAEL: I've been living a lie for you! I did everything your damn way!!!

DAWN: [*overlapping, sudden realisation*] Oh no! The baby!

DEBBIE: What?

DAWN: [*to* MICHAEL] What's going to happen to your poor little baby?!

MICHAEL: It's all right Mum. Monique's not pregnant.

DAWN: She's not?

MICHAEL: She's not.

RON: Then why did you tell me she was?

MICHAEL: I *didn't!*

DAWN: There's no baby…?

MICHAEL: That's right. There's no baby.

KAREN: There's no baby?

MICHAEL: Yes! There's *no* baby!

DEBBIE: Actually—there *is* a baby.

MICHAEL: Debbie, you of all people should know—we're not—

RON: [*interrupting*] Michael was just having a joke with us Debbie. You poofters have got a strange sense of humour.

DAWN: So I'm not going to be a grandma.

DEBBIE: Yes Mum. You *are*—(going to be a grandma)

MICHAEL: [*interrupting impatiently*] How many times do I have to say this? Monique and me are *not* having a baby!
DEBBIE: *I'm* having a baby. [*Beat.*] *I* am. [*Beat.*] *I'm* pregnant.
DAWN/RON/MICHAEL/KAREN: What?! / *You're* pregnant?! [*Etc.*]
DEBBIE: I wasn't going to tell anyone yet... I'm eleven weeks.
DAWN/KAREN: [*in unison*] You're... pregnant?

    DEBBIE *nods.*

MICHAEL: Why didn't you tell me?
RON: So you *have* got a fella?
DEBBIE: For God's sake, Dad.

    Beat. They all stare at her.

Look. I wasn't planning for this to happen, but it did, and now that I'm used to the idea... I'm really quite excited about it.
MICHAEL: Was it Jeff?

    DEBBIE *nods.*

KAREN: Who's Jeff?

    DEBBIE *remains silent.*

Nobody tells me anything.
DEBBIE: There's nothing to tell. It's over.
RON: Don't be stupid. You'll have to marry the bloke.
DEBBIE: I can't marry him. I don't love him.
DAWN: But Debbie, you must have. You... had *sex* with him.
DEBBIE: Mum. It's 2003.
RON: What's that got to do with anything? You'll have to marry the bloke to give the baby a home.
DEBBIE: I'm not getting married.
RON: Yes you bloody are!
DEBBIE: No I'm bloody not!
MICHAEL: Great. You want her to do the same thing I did: waste years of her life and somebody else's being totally miserable! [*Beat.*] Let me tell you something Dad: Marriage sucks!
DAWN: Karen. Don't listen to your brother and sister. Marriage is a beautiful institution.
RON: Michael's marriage is a unique and—perverted situation. And Debbie's being extremely selfish. Marriage is a wonderful thing.

Look at me and your mother—
KAREN: Oh, don't give me that!

They all look at her in surprise.

Everything has to go *your* way, Dad. Every little thing. And Mum tiptoes around you like a frightened mouse. [*Beat.*] If Craig and I thought *that* was marriage, we'd never do it in a million years!

DAWN *and* RON *are astounded by* KAREN's *words. She takes a few deep breaths, regains her composure.*

I don't like being rude to my elders, but that had to be said. Maybe we should move on to the next item?

END OF ACT ONE

ACT TWO

The stage is in darkness.

The tick tick of the clock is now joined by a knock knock to the same beat. We may or may not realise they are separate sounds. The slide projector is turned on. Onto the now blank light on the wall a slide is projected. It's hastily and untidily scrawled. It reads: Late Unscheduled Item: Very Private Moments–Ron.

The lights come up to reveal RON *standing on a chair in the middle of the living room. He has made a noose and is trying to tie it up to a light fitting above his head. The noose is not around his neck as yet.*

The knock knocking coming from the kitchen, increases in tempo and urgency.

KAREN: [*through door*] Dad let us in!
DEBBIE: [*through door*] We didn't mean it!
MICHAEL: [*through door*] You're a wonderful father!
RON: I'm a lousy father. You said so.
DEBBIE: [*through door*] We never used that exact terminology.
KAREN: [*through door*] I didn't mean what I said about you and Mum!
DEBBIE: [*through door*] I didn't mean what I said about things being your fault!
MICHAEL: [*through door*] I was joking, Dad!

    RON *stops for a moment.*

RON: You were joking?
MICHAEL: [*through door*] Yeah.
RON: About *everything?*
MICHAEL: [*through door*] Well. Almost. Except the homosexual bit.

    RON *goes back to securing the noose.*

RON: I want you kids to leave me alone now.
KAREN: [*hisses at* MICHAEL *through door*] Tell him you're not gay!
MICHAEL: [*hisses back*] I can't.
KAREN: [*hisses*] It's only for another thirty-nine minutes.

MICHAEL: [*hisses*] I'm not going to!
KAREN: [*hisses*] If Debbie asked you to do it you would!
DEBBIE: [*hisses*] For God's sake Karen. This is hardly the time.

> *Unseen by* RON, DAWN *enters from the other side of the room carrying two cups of steaming black coffee.* DAWN *has sobered up considerably. She's behind* RON. *She reacts at seeing him tying the noose, then composes herself.*

[*Calling through door*] Dad. What are you doing in there?
RON: I told you. I've scheduled some private moments for myself.
KAREN: [*through door*] Are you all right?
RON: Physically, I'm well-equipped to live until ten twenty-three. Emotionally, it's another story. [*Sighs.*] But that's something I hold myself entirely responsible for. And I want you kids to know that if by some chance I don't make it to the appointed hour…

> *He grunts as he fastens a difficult knot.*

Euggh.

> MICHAEL, DEBBIE *and* KAREN *are frantic at these ominous words.*

KAREN: [*hisses*] He's killing himself!
DEBBIE: [*overlapping*] We've got to do something!
DEBBIE & KAREN: Michael! Do something!

> MICHAEL *knocks loudly on the door.*

MICHAEL: [*through door*] If you don't let us in we'll knock the door down!
RON: Just leave me in peace.
KAREN: [*through door*] But what are you doing?!
DAWN: Your father's got himself all in knots. And you lot yelling through the door isn't helping.

> RON *turns to look at* DAWN.

MICHAEL: [*hisses, relieved*] Mum's in there.
DEBBIE: [*overlapping*] Thank God!
KAREN: [*through door*] Mum we think Dad's going to—
DAWN: [*interrupting, calling*] That's enough Karen. I want you all to respect your father's wishes for a few Private Moments.
KAREN: [*through door*] Sorry Mum.
DEBBIE: [*through door*] Sorry Dad.

MICHAEL: [*through door*] Sorry.
DAWN: There'll be plenty of time for sorries later.
> *The tick tick of the clock reminds everyone that time may be the last thing they have.*
> ~~Just leave Dad alone for a bit.~~
> ~~MICHAEL/DEBBIE/KAREN: Okay. / Yeah. / Of course. / Sorry. [Etc.]~~
> *Then silence from the kitchen.*

RON: How did you get in here?
DAWN: I've got a spare key to the front door, as if you didn't know.
> RON *ignores the implications of* DAWN's *words. They both stare up at the noose.*

RON: Oh, I'm sorry. I know this is a cowardly act. I was going to leave you a farewell note… but you can never find a biro in this bloody place.
> DAWN *pushes a cup of black coffee towards* RON.

DAWN: Have one of these, Ron. I've had four. It's sobered me up well and truly.
> RON *waves the coffee away, dramatically disgusted.*

RON: I'm not *drunk*, Dawn. I'm a failure as a father. And a cup of coffee's going to do bugger-all to fix that. [*Beat.*] No, there's only one way. I have to end it.
> *They both look up at the noose.* RON *sneaks a peak at her.*

DAWN: Well that knot won't do the trick.
> *Pushes him off chair.*

Here. Let me try. I think I remember from Girl Guides.
> DAWN *climbs up onto the chair and starts adjusting the knot.*

RON: Dawn…?
DAWN: What you need is a reef knot.
> RON *watches her in silent amazement, then…*

RON: And you reckon you're sober?
DAWN: You've only got half an hour left anyway. It's six of one half a dozen of the other.
RON: I have to do it.

DAWN: I couldn't agree more.
RON: I can't live with my failure.
DAWN: And why should you, Ron? You've had thirty-five years to be a half-hearted father. You've got thirty-five minutes to try and make up for it. And that might mean saying sorry. And listening. You're right. It's too hard. Go ahead. Kill yourself.
RON: I *wanted* to get to know them better. I wanted to know what they were thinking and feeling. I wanted—
DAWN: [*interrupting*] You wanted them to pat you on the back and lie about how wonderful you are. But they didn't. And now you're sulking.

> DAWN *looks at* RON *challengingly. Silence. She's not going to make this easy for him.*

RON: Dawn. Our son is a *homosexual*.
DAWN: [*finds this difficult*] Yes he is.
RON: That *must* mean I've stuffed up.
DAWN: Maybe it does.
RON: And do you think it's my fault that Debbie's got a baby on the way but no bloke to go with it?
DAWN: *She* seems to think so.
RON: Have I really been… *emotionally unavailable?*
DAWN: So she says.

> RON *looks at* DAWN *in surprise.*

RON: You're not even trying to cheer me up.
DAWN: I'm tired of cheering you up Ron. You've got such a small amount of time left and you're trying to waste it on this pointless conversation because you're too scared to face your children.

> RON *reacts to* DAWN*'s stern tone with pride.*

RON: [*teases*] And Karen thinks *you're* frightened of *me*.

> DAWN *simply smiles.* RON *holds out his hand and helps* DAWN *off the chair in an old-fashioned, chivalrous gesture.*

Have I really been such a lousy husband?
DAWN: Now you want *me* to tell lies about how wonderful you are.
RON: Come on… couldn't you tell me *one?*

> RON *and* DAWN *share a tender smile.*

DAWN: It's funny. They think it stops, don't they? Kids. They think you stop feeling all of those things.
RON: I'm going to miss you Dawnie.
DAWN: I'll miss you too.

> *They move into a gentle kiss, then a warm and lingering hug. As they break apart...*

RON: I'll let 'em in, eh...?

> RON *moves over to the kitchen door. He opens it and...* MICHAEL, DEBBIE *and* KAREN *fall through into the living room. They've been straining at the door, trying to eavesdrop.*

MICHAEL/DEBBIE/KAREN: Oooh! / Aaggh! / We were just—
RON: You can come in now.

> *The kids cluster around* RON. DAWN *watches on.*

KAREN: Dad. Thank God you're... (okay)

> *She stops as she notices something.* DEBBIE *and* MICHAEL *follow her gaze to the noose, still hanging from the ceiling. A very awkward silence, then all at once...*

I'm sorry I said that stuff about marriage. Everybody's different and just because I don't want me and Craig to be like you and Mum doesn't give me—(the right...)
DEBBIE: And I'm sorry I blamed you for me being single. I'm an adult and I have to take responsibility for my own life and if I've got some kind of problem—(it's up to me to work it out)
MICHAEL: And I shouldn't have tried to hit you but I was confused and when you wouldn't drink out of my glass I felt so hurt that—(I lashed out)

> DEBBIE, MICHAEL *and* KAREN *have all been speaking at the same time.*
>
> RON *holds up his arms to silence them.*

RON: [*whistles loudly*] Hey. Hey. Woah.

> *They stop. Silence for a beat, then...*

KAREN: I'm sorrier than them, Dad. I'm the sorriest!
RON: If anyone should be making amends around here, it's *me*. [*Beat.*] Saying sor... admitting that I've been in the wrong doesn't come

easy to me. A man doesn't like to acknowledge that he could have handled things better. But that's obviously, *very obviously*, the case in my case… so…

KAREN/MICHAEL/DEBBIE: It's okay Dad. / Don't… you know. / You don't have to say sorry… [*Etc.*]

RON: [*interrupting*] No. Hear me out.

>*Pause.*

I want to say that I regret my—I'm *sorry* for all my inadequacies as a father. And I love you and respect you all very much—regardless of your marital status, pregnancy situation or sexual preference.

MICHAEL/DEBBIE/KAREN: Oh Dad… / Dad… / Oh…

DAWN: Oh Ron, Darling…

RON: [*holds out his arms*] How about a hug?

>*They all move hesitantly and awkwardly into a communal hug.*

>DEBBIE *is about to hug* RON *when* KAREN *practically pushes her out of the way to get closest to him.* DAWN *joins in.* MICHAEL *is last to join the hug. He walks towards the group with his arms outstretched tentatively.*

[*reaches for him*] Son.

>MICHAEL *joins in and the family is one hybrid embracing beast.*

>*A knock at the front door.*

>*They all remain rooted together, not wanting to break the moment. A beat or two.*

>*Another knock at the front door.*

EVERYONE: [*in unison*] I'll get it.

>*Shared laughter.*

RON: I tell you what. We'll *all* get it.

>*The strange hybrid embracing beast moves as one towards the front door. Then* DEBBIE'*s back goes again.*

DEBBIE: Oooh!

RON: Are you all right Debbie?

DAWN: Is it your tummy?

DEBBIE: No. It's my back again.

DAWN: You'll have to be careful now you're having a baby…

As everyone else gathers around DEBBIE, MICHAEL *walks to the front door and opens it. A good-looking young man in a dark suit stands on the threshold. He has a polite, puppy-dog eagerness and carries a briefcase. He's* TED WILKINS.

MICHAEL: Hello.

TED: Good evening. [*Holds out his hand.*] My name's Ted Wilkins, from Wilkins and Son Funeral Directors.

A dazed MICHAEL *shakes his hand.*

May I offer my sincere condolences.

Looks around the room.

To the entire family.

RON *approaches and shakes* TED's *hand.*

Note: TED *does* not *notice the noose.*

RON: Ted. Pleased to meet you in person.

TED: Perhaps you could take me to the deceased.

RON: *I'm* the deceased.

TED: But you're not deceased.

RON: I won't be deceased until ten twenty-three.

TED: But it's— [*Looks at his watch.*] eleven-o-seven.

RON: No. It's nine fifty-seven.

TED: No. It's eleven—

He looks at the clock on the wall, realises.

Oh. I'm terribly sorry. I've still got my watch set on Daylight Saving.

He gives another polite smile around the room.

Guess I'll just have to wait then.

TED *plonks himself down on a chair. They all stare at him.*

Please don't let me intrude. Just go on with whatever you were doing.

Another non-plussed silence. Then DAWN *picks up a plate from the table and proffers it to* TED.

DAWN: Can I offer you a Salada?

TED: [*takes one with a polite smile*] Thank you.

RON: Ted. This is Dawn Patterson. The best wife a man ever had.

DAWN: Oh, Ron...
TED: I'm delighted to meet you Mrs Patterson.
DAWN: And these are our three kids. We might have had our differences in the past—some people were more aware of them than others—but I'm pleased to say we've patched things up in plenty of time for the funeral.

> TED *smiles with polite interest.*

RON: This is Karen. The baby of the family. She's getting married soon.
TED: Oh. Please accept my congratulations along with my condolences.
KAREN: Thank you.
RON: But she's doing it *her* way Ted. She's learning from me and her mother's mistakes, and *she's* going to be the boss!
KAREN: I didn't mean that Dad. I got carried away. It was Michael and Debbie's fault. They made me—
RON: Sssh. Hey. I respect you for having an opinion, Princess. And this is our eldest daughter. Debbie.

> *He squeezes* DEBBIE. *It hurts her back. She winces.*

DEBBIE: Hi.
TED: Nice to meet you.
RON: Debbie's single.
TED: [*polite*] Oh?
RON: And she's having a baby.
DEBBIE: Dad!
RON: [*jovial*] She slept with a bloke but she didn't love him.

> TED *nods politely.*

A lot of girls do that these days. Debbie's got a wonderful job and lots of close friends. And hobbies and so on. Her life's very fulfilled.

> TED *nods again.*

Dawn and I are extremely proud of her. Especially *me*. And I'm interested in everything she does. No matter how small or insignificant.
TED: Well. It must be nice to have such an attentive father.

> RON *squeezes* DEBBIE *again. She winces in pain.*

RON: And that handsome bloke over there is my son, Michael.
TED: We met at the door. Hello again.

IT'S MY PARTY (AND I'LL DIE IF I WANT TO) 145

> RON *puts his arm around* MICHAEL *and* MICHAEL *realises with horror what he is about to say as...*

RON: Michael's a homosexual.

> *Stunned silence. Except from* MICHAEL.

MICHAEL: Christ.

RON: But it makes no difference to me and Dawn. We still love him just as much.

> TED *nods politely.*

And he loves a bloke called Alex! Don't you?

MICHAEL: Andrew.

RON: Yeah. Of course. Absolutely. Shame I'll never get to meet the man who makes my son so happy.

> *He's trying so hard to be cool about this, but finding it very difficult.*

Tell us a bit about him, Michael. How did you two fellas get together?

> MICHAEL *looks towards* DAWN. *This is hardly an appropriate time or place.*

MICHAEL: Dad...

RON: [*follows his gaze*] No. Come on. Your mother's just as interested as I am.

DAWN: [*supportive smile to* MICHAEL] Of course I am Sweetheart.

RON: We're all interested. Aren't we? [*Beat.*] Girls?

DEBBIE: Absolutely.

KAREN: You may as well tell us.

> MICHAEL *looks hesitantly towards* TED.

TED: Please. Don't mind me.

MICHAEL: Well, he's been a colleague for a few years. But we were working late one night last month and... [*Smiles at the memory.*] He kissed me. That was the night we became lovers.

> *At the word "lovers"* RON *nearly has a fit. He tries to hide it with a huge phoney smile.*

RON: R-i-i-i-g-h-t! How about another cuppa? Dawn, I'll give you a hand.

> RON *exits into the kitchen as fast as his legs will carry him, dragging* DAWN *behind.*

DAWN: [*to* TED] Excuse me a moment, Ted.

> RON *and* DAWN *exit.*

TED: I must say it's very refreshing to meet such an open and communicative family.

KAREN: Oh, Dad's always been pretty relaxed about that sort of stuff.

From the kitchen we hear...

DAWN: Ron, calm down! You're hyper-ventilating!

> KAREN *looks at* MICHAEL *in annoyance, forgetting* TED *for a moment.*

KAREN: You shouldn't have told him.

MICHAEL: He had to find out sometime.

KAREN: But he didn't have to find out *tonight!*

MICHAEL: We all have to hear things we don't want to hear Karen.

KAREN: You're just selfish.

DEBBIE: Karen—

KAREN: [*interrupting*] And so are you, Debbie. You two think you're so smart with all your little secrets.

DEBBIE: Oh, here we go.

MICHAEL: Why are you so paranoid?

KAREN: I'm not paranoid. You never tell me anything. But you tell each other *everything.*

MICHAEL: Debbie didn't tell me she was having a baby.

KAREN: Huh. Debbie shouldn't be having a baby.

> DEBBIE *looks at* KAREN *in disbelief.*

You've got no respect for the father, whoever he is, and you'll have no support with the poor little child—

DEBBIE: Karen, don't you think that's *my*—(business?)

KAREN: [*yells*] And you're going to be fat at my wedding!

A few beats as she calms herself down.

You're going to be an unmarried mother, Debbie. How do you think that makes Dad feel?

DEBBIE: How about how *I* feel?

KAREN: How *you* feel doesn't matter. Dad just might be dying tonight!

MICHAEL: He's not going to die.

TED: But he rang and booked.

They all look at him, suddenly remembering his presence.

MICHAEL: I'm afraid we're probably wasting your time Ted.

DEBBIE: But if we are, Michael and I will give you some compensation for—

KAREN: *I'll* give him some money too.

DEBBIE: But Karen. You're always saying you have to save for the wedding.

KAREN: Why do you always have to bring up my wedding? They just want to spoil it for me, Ted.

DEBBIE: [*turns to* TED] What did I say? Did I sound like I wanted to spoil it to you?

TED: [*tries to stay neutral*] Well, I—

MICHAEL: [*interrupting*] You've got problems, Karen. [*To* TED.] Wouldn't you say so?

KAREN *taps* TED *on the shoulder to get his attention.*

KAREN: They hate me because they think I'm Dad's favourite.

DEBBIE: You *are* Dad's favourite.

MICHAEL: She's definitely his favourite.

TED: Your father doesn't seem to have a favourite to me. He's very loving with all of you.

KAREN: See? See?

MICHAEL: Ted. Let me set you straight on a few things here. I bet you thought Dad's known I'm gay for years? That he's been comfortable with it since 1987 or some bloody thing. Right?

TED: Well, yes, I did think that…

MICHAEL: And I don't blame you Ted. Because the man you've met tonight bears *no resemblance* to the father we've had for thirty-five years.

TED: That seems a little harsh to me—

DEBBIE: It's not Ted. Michael's telling the truth. You haven't seen what Dad's really like.

TED: I've seen enough to know that he's an emotionally open and loving man.

RON *re-enters. He's sewn his smile back on.*

RON: Well. Dawn seems to have the tea under control. [*Smile to* MICHAEL.] Lovers, eh? That's, ah… yeah, terrific.

> MICHAEL *squirms under* RON's *ultra-"relaxed" smile.*
>
> *The tick tick of the clock.*

TED: Mr Patterson. I wonder if you'd be interested in taking this opportunity to participate in a few decisions about your funeral? I usually discuss these matters with close relatives post-death, but seeing we've got about [*Looks to clock*] twenty-five minutes prior to the cessation of life, I thought you might like to be involved.

RON: Why not?

> *Beaming excitedly from ear to ear,* TED *moves to his briefcase and opens it.*

TED: I've never dealt directly with the deceased before, so I hope you'll bear with me while I feel my way.

> RON *glances at the clock as* TED *rummages in his briefcase.*

RON: Take your time Ted. No pressure.

TED: Now Mr Patterson...

> DAWN *re-enters with a tray full of tea cups.*

The first thing I have to do is measure you for your coffin.

DAWN: He's five feet ten inches. Has been since the day I first met him at the ice skating rink in 1967. My lace was undone. Ron offered to tie it. [*Smiles.*] Five feet ten, Ted.

> DAWN *hands out tea cups. Ad-lib thank you's, etc.*

TED: I don't mean to doubt your word Mrs Patterson, but sometimes as people get older and life's worries take their toll, they can start to lose an inch or two...

RON: After all the things I've found out tonight I'm probably four foot eleven then!

> *They all laugh a tad uncomfortably.* RON *nudges* MICHAEL.

Just a joke Son. I'm completely comfortable with your lifestyle. And very supportive.

MICHAEL: Thanks Dad.

TED: I seem to have left my tape measure back at the morgue. Would you have some string, or... *rope* perhaps...?

> *As* TED *is speaking he moves to a point where he is standing*

directly under the noose. An embarrassed reaction from the Pattersons as they look up at it.

RON: Well, what do you know? We do have some… ah, rope.

TED follows RON's gaze and gulps down his tea in shock at the sight of the noose. RON starts to carry a chair over to the noose. KAREN takes it from him.

KAREN: Here Dad. I'll do that.

RON: Thanks, Sweetie.

They all watch uncomfortably as KAREN climbs onto the chair and unties the noose. Another silence. Then…

DAWN: Ted? How's your tea?

TED: [*shell-shocked*] Delicious thank you, Mrs Patterson.

DEBBIE shoves a plate of Saladas in front of him.

DEBBIE: Salada?

TED: Ah, I hope you won't think that I'm being presumptuous, but I'd just like to say that I really think you're quite a remarkable family unit.

DAWN: Thank you Ted.

TED: If all families could be as open as yours, funerals would be a lot more fun to attend. [*Beat.*] —Ah, not that they're supposed to be fun, of course.

KAREN is off the chair. She hands TED the rope.

KAREN: Here Ted.

TED: Thank you. [*Turns to RON.*] What I'll do is get you to stand up straight Mr Patterson, and if someone could hold the bottom of the rope while I measure it up to your height and mark it.

TED reaches into his suit pocket and gets out a pen as MICHAEL takes the bottom of the rope.

MICHAEL: Here… I'll do it.

MICHAEL holds the rope near the bottom of RON's foot.

RON: You right there Son? [*Jovial.*] Keep away from that inside leg!

MICHAEL grimaces in irritation.

Just a little joke.

MICHAEL: Right Dad...

> MICHAEL's *mobile phone starts ringing.*

Excuse me. Here, Deb.

> DEBBIE *takes* MICHAEL's *end of the rope while* MICHAEL *moves off to answer his phone call. Meanwhile* TED *takes the other end of the rope and holds it up against* RON.

[*into phone*] Michael Patterson. Yeah Phil. What did they say? Christ! What have you got for ears? Russian roubles?! Tell them that's not enough! [*Etc.*]

> *As* MICHAEL's *conversation continues...*

DAWN: Are you sure you should be crouching, Debbie? Maybe Karen could...

DEBBIE: [*good-natured*] I'm pregnant Mum. I'm not an invalid.

KAREN: Yeah. She's not an invalid.

RON: What about your back? Is it giving you trouble?

DEBBIE: No. It's fine at the moment Dad.

KAREN: *Mine's* hurting a bit.

RON: Oh Sweetie...

DEBBIE: Since when?

> TED *is holding his end of the rope up against* RON's *head with a biro in the other hand, but as* RON *won't keep his head still, the measuring process is proving a difficult task.* TED *is starting to feel a tad put out.*

TED: Please...

DAWN: Stand up straight Ron. If you slump you'll be shorter than five foot ten and you don't want to feel cramped in your coffin.

TED: [*marks the rope with biro*] Right. Got that. Thanks Mr Patterson.

> TED *takes the rope and starts rolling it.* DEBBIE *rolls from the other end. They meet in the middle.* RON *looks on.*

RON: You know, you two look great together. Don't they Dawn?

DEBBIE: Dad...

RON: Are you married, Ted?

TED: [*putting the rope in his briefcase*] No I'm not.

> RON *raises his eyebrows significantly at* DEBBIE.

RON: Like babies, do you?
DAWN: Ron. Ssssh...

TED picks up a folder from his briefcase.

TED: Now you might like to choose a coffin. I have photographs of the different styles and finishes we offer. If you'd all like to gather around...
DAWN: Michael. Come and help us, Sweetheart.

MICHAEL wanders over and stands behind the couch, looking over people's heads at the coffin photos while still conducting his telephone conversation.

Meanwhile RON pushes DEBBIE towards TED.

RON: Debbie. You're chief advisor. [*To* TED.] Debbie knows a lot about styles and finishes. She's an interior designer.
TED: Oh?
RON: A talented one too. We're all very proud.

TED registers this with a polite smile.

KAREN: Are you prouder of Debbie than you are of me?
DAWN: Dad's proud of you all exactly the same. Aren't you Ron?
RON: Spot-on Dawn. Isn't that so Ted?
TED: It certainly seems that way to me.

He turns his attention back to the folder.

We start off with the basic model; which is comprised of particle board with unlaquered finish. And the handles and personally engraved plaque are gold-plated.

The family gazes at the photograph in the folder.

KAREN: It looks cheap.
MICHAEL: No style.
DAWN: Not shiny enough.
RON: [*to* TED] Debbie's a good cook too—and you should see her flat—always spick and span...

DEBBIE nudges her mother sharply: Help me!

DAWN: Now Ron. Pay attention to the coffins. *You're* the one who has to live in the thing.

DAWN laughs at her unconscious pun. Everyone joins in.

Live in it! Ooh, that's funny. Anyway. Pay attention.

RON *throws his arm around* DAWN *and turns to* KAREN.

RON: And you think *I* give the orders!
KAREN: [*feels guilty*] Dad... (I didn't mean that)
DAWN: It's all right Sweetheart. We know you didn't mean any harm.
RON: You were concerned. And no wonder. You're about to take that big step yourself. Did I tell you Karen's getting married Ted?
TED: Yes you did. Congratulations again.
RON: If you're thinking she looks younger than Debbie, you're right. There's eight years between them. Debbie's thirty-two.
TED: Really?
RON: But as far as we're concerned she's still a spring chicken. And we're proud of the fact that she's single.

TED *nods with a smile.*

And pregnant.

DEBBIE *is incredibly mortified.*

Have you got a girlfriend, Ted?
DEBBIE: Can we move onto the next coffin?
TED: [*referring back to his folder*] Of course. This model comes in teak, with a natural stain finish...
MICHAEL: [*into telephone*] All right. I'll hold.

MICHAEL *starts looking at the coffins with slightly more interest.*

DAWN: [*peers at it*] That's quite nice...
DEBBIE: It doesn't look well-finished to me...
RON: Oh. I think it—(does) Ah. Never mind.
DEBBIE: What?
RON: Nothing.
TED: Then there's the cedar coffin with natural polish.

Everyone murmurs in approval.

It's a middle of the road model that's a popular choice for the deceased we deal with. Those handles come in silver or gold.
DEBBIE: That's better.
DAWN: It looks dignified.
MICHAEL: I don't mind that.
KAREN: I like it.

MICHAEL: [*into phone*] Yeah Phil. I'm here.

He turns away and resumes his conversation.

A silence as the others wait for RON *to express his opinion on the cedar coffin.*

DAWN: Ron? What do you think?

RON: I'm leaving the decision up to Debbie. She's the decor expert in the family.

DEBBIE: You're sure you trust my decisions?

RON: Completely.

DEBBIE: Then we'll take that one. With gold handles.

RON: Silver.

DEBBIE: What?

RON: Just a suggestion.

DEBBIE: See? You *don't* trust me!

RON: I trust you! [*To* TED.] Gold.

DEBBIE: No. He wants silver.

RON: No. I want gold.

DEBBIE: He's lying.

RON: I'm not lying. I want gold.

DAWN: But Ron—you did say silver.

RON: I've changed my mind. I want gold.

DAWN: But you don't like gold.

RON: I love gold.

DAWN: No you don't.

RON: *I'm* the corpse. *I* know what I want on my coffin!

MICHAEL: [*trying to hear on phone*] Sssssh!

DEBBIE: I can't do anything right by you, can I? Nothing I do is right!

DAWN: Now Debbie…

DEBBIE: You said you're sorry and you want to take an interest, but you still can't trust me, can you?!

DAWN: Think of the baby, Darling.

DEBBIE: You keep saying you're proud but you don't mean it. You won't even let me pick your coffin handles!

MICHAEL: Ssssh!

RON: I'm letting you pick them! *Gold* for Christ's sake!

DEBBIE: And you say you couldn't care less that I'm single, but all you've been doing for the last fifteen minutes is trying to set me up with an *undertaker!* [*Turns to* TED.] No offence Ted.

TED: [*crestfallen*] None taken.

DEBBIE: You either ignore me or pick-pick-pick. It has to be one or the other. You think I'm stupid don't you? You—

RON: No Debbie. *I'm* the stupid one.

DEBBIE: You got *that* right.

KAREN: Debbie! Mum—did you hear that?!

> MICHAEL *gives* KAREN *a disparaging look as* RON *moves over and puts his arm around* DEBBIE.

RON: Your sister's spot-on Karen. Sometimes your old dad's a few kangaroos short in the top paddock.

DEBBIE: Oh, I didn't mean it…

RON: No. You're absolutely right. I was being a dill. [*Beat.*] Silver'd tarnish anyway, Sweetie.

> DEBBIE *recognises the backdown for the apology and concession it is. She smiles as* RON *kisses the top of her head. A reconciliation. A real one.* RON *squeezes her tight.* KAREN *watches, miffed.*

MICHAEL: Well fix it Phil! Or the only thing you'll be dealing—is, is—a pack of cards!

> MICHAEL *hangs up, quite pleased with his spur-of-the-moment threat.*

> *The tick tick of the clock.*

> *They all look to the wall.*

KAREN: Fifteen minutes.

> *She virtually pulls* DEBBIE *and* RON *apart.*

Oh Dad, I can't believe you'll be gone so soon.

RON: Fifteen minutes and it'll all be over.

DAWN: Don't say that, Ron. It'll just be beginning.

> *Beat.* RON *looks unconvinced.*

It *will.* You'll be going on a new and wonderful journey…

RON: Yeah. All the way from here to the cemetery. And instead of a bus I'll be catching a coffin, eh Ted?

DAWN: No Ron—you'll float down a long white tunnel—and Grandad

IT'S MY PARTY (AND I'LL DIE IF I WANT TO)

will be at the end, waiting for you with his arms wide open!
KAREN: Oh Mum, do you think so...?
DAWN: [*nods*] Of course I do. And Grandma Hurley will be there too—
KAREN: Oh, and Soxy! Do you think Dad will see Soxy again?
DAWN: Of course he will.

> MICHAEL *and* DEBBIE *also have very fond memories of Soxy.*

MICHAEL/DEBBIE: Oh, good old Soxy. / I'd love to see Soxy...
RON: Who the hell is Soxy?
DAWN: That labrador we had for eleven years, Ron.
RON: Oh yeah. Right. Of course.
DAWN: Will you give Grandma Hurley a great big hug for me and tell her I found her brooch behind the kitchen cabinet?
RON: I will if I see her.
DAWN: Of course you'll see her.
RON: I'm not making any promises, Dawn. It depends on life after death.
DAWN: I wish you'd have more faith Ron. There *is* life after death. There *is*.
RON: [*tries to joke*] I'll let you know.
KAREN: Oh, could you, Dad? [*Beat.*] We could think of a signal. So we know your spirit's here with us.

> *Shocked reactions around the room.*

MICHAEL: Karen. That is the most spastic idea—
RON: I like the idea. Ted, would you have an ethical problem with that?
TED: Not at all!
RON: Well. I tell you what. I'll knock like this— [*Demonstrates a distinct knocking pattern.*] and then I'll smash [*Points.*] *The Bounty*.
DAWN: Oh Ron, not *The Bounty*.
RON: All right. I won't smash anything. But I'll knock like this— [*Demonstrates knocking pattern again.*] If you hear that you'll know I'm in the room. Got it?

> *They all nod with varying degrees of discomfort.* DAWN *doesn't like talking about this stuff.*

DAWN: Ah Ted, perhaps we should get back to the funeral arrangements?
TED: Well, maybe we could move onto the topic of hymns for the service. Strictly speaking this is the minister's domain, but considering that I'm here and so are you, Mr Patterson...

RON: I want them to sing my favourite song.
KAREN: Dad you can't sing *What's New Pussycat?* at a funeral.
RON: Tom Jones. You know it?
TED: [*gets a hymn book from his briefcase*] It's probably more appropriate to choose a hymn from the traditional selections—
RON: I don't give a rat's ring what's appropriate Ted.
DAWN: Ron!
RON: Is it appropriate for Karen to tell me and Dawn how we should conduct our marriage?
KAREN: Dad—
RON: Is it appropriate for Debbie to be carrying the kid of some bloke she's hardly clapped eyes on—?
DEBBIE: Dad—
RON: Is it appropriate for Michael to be kissing some fella behind the photocopier—?
DAWN: Ron, please. You're being ill-mannered.
TED: [*ever polite*] It's all right Mrs Patterson. I take your husband's point.

Makes a note in his folder.

We'll see what we can do.
RON: And I want Michael to sing it.
MICHAEL: What?
RON: Solo.
MICHAEL: You're kidding.
RON: You're my only son. That's the way I want it.
MICHAEL: You've got to be off your rocker.
RON: Just gird your loins and go for it, Son.
MICHAEL: I'm not going to sing *What's New Pussycat?* at your funeral.
RON: Of course you are.
MICHAEL: No I'm not.

    RON *starts wheezing for effect.*

DAWN: Michael. If it's what your father wants…
KAREN: [*overlapping*] It wouldn't kill you to do this one little thing.
DEBBIE: [*overlapping*] It'll be over in a minute. It won't be that bad—
MICHAEL: But I've got the worst singing voice in the world!
RON: Rubbish. All you homosexual fellas can sing. And dance. And write poetry.

MICHAEL: That's the most ignorant—(generalisation etc)
DEBBIE: Maybe we should move along. Ted. What else do we need to decide?
TED: I'd like to have a general idea about numbers. Now I'm assuming that the first two pews will be taken up with relatives. Is that a safe assumption?
RON: That depends on whether Lorraine and Barry are there.
DAWN: She's your sister Ron. Of course she'll be there.
RON: But they're up in Surfers. [*To* TED, *by way of explanation.*] I was going to warn her about the funeral but she's got her heart set on seeing *Movie World*.

    TED *nods understandingly.*

DAWN: We'll make up at least the first pew anyway. Debbie and me, and Karen and Matthew, and Michael and Monique—
RON: And Angus.
MICHAEL: It's Andrew.
RON: Yeah.
MICHAEL: [*overlapping*] But he won't be there.
RON: Why not?
MICHAEL: Oh come on.
RON: He's the man you love isn't he? Surely he could come along to offer you some emotional support...?

    RON *tries not to wince.*

You'll need a hand to hold... a comforting... cuddle.
MICHAEL: Dad. Monique will be there.
RON: You said Monique knows about him.
MICHAEL: She does. But that doesn't make it appropriate.
RON: Have you had ear muffs on Mate? I don't care what's appropriate anymore.
MICHAEL: [*sighs heavily*] Dad. It's not a good idea for me to bring Monique *and* Andrew to your funeral.
RON: But she knows about him.
MICHAEL: That doesn't mean she likes it!
RON: She may not like it but she'll have to get used to it.
MICHAEL: It's not that simple.
RON: Yes it is. Your mother and me have managed.
MICHAEL: Monique's in a lot of pain, Dad.

RON: We all feel for her Son. But she'll just have to take a leaf out of my book and come to terms with the situation.
MICHAEL: Oh don't give me that bullshit!
DAWN: Michael!
MICHAEL: The only thing you've ever come to terms with is the sound of your own voice!

Shocked reactions from the family.

I wish I'd never told you I was gay! At least when we were lying we were being honest!
RON: Now Mate. Don't you start that kind of—
MICHAEL: [*interrupting*] You don't understand it. You don't respect it. So for Christ's sake stop pretending that you do!
KAREN: Dad's just being supportive Michael.
MICHAEL: Bullshit Karen. He's fucking performing!
DAWN: Don't use that language in this house!
MICHAEL: I'm sorry Mum, but that's how I feel.
DAWN: Your father's doing his best…
KAREN: It isn't easy for men Dad's age…
DEBBIE: I know he's hopeless, but he *is* genuinely trying…
TED: Your father's making a very real effort Michael.

A short silence.

MICHAEL: If he's really making such an effort—*Ted*—why hasn't he taken me aside? Why hasn't he asked me anything about it? [*Looks to clock.*] You think you're going to be dead in eleven minutes, and you haven't spent two seconds alone with me since you found out. You haven't bothered to *ask* me what it means.

RON is genuinely repentant.

RON: I'm sorry Son. Let's do that now, then. Let's talk about this. Together. Alone.
DAWN: That's a lovely idea. We'll leave you to it, then.

DAWN, KAREN and DEBBIE exit to the kitchen. DAWN turns at the doorway.

Don't be too long Sweethearts. Time's running out.

RON and MICHAEL are about to have a heart to heart when they realise that TED is still present, eagerly and supportively anticipating their reconciliation. He's watching them with interest. They are non-plussed. DAWN *pops her head back in.*

Ted. Would you like to help us wash up some tea cups?

TED *shakes his head in a polite refusal. A more pointed look from* DAWN *and then he realises, getting to his feet.*

TED: What a good idea Mrs Patterson. People will no doubt be dropping in to offer their condolences.

TED *follows* DAWN *into the kitchen. On the way out he turns and gives* RON *a crossed-fingers, good luck gesture.*

DAWN *and* TED *exit.*

RON *and* MICHAEL *stand facing each other, about to communicate for the first time ever. A short silence, then...*

RON: Well Son. I'm here, and I'm listening. Tell me how you feel.

After a long silence...

MICHAEL: I feel—

MICHAEL*'s mobile phone rings.*

Damn! Excuse me. [*Into phone.*] Michael Patterson. Oh. Hi. You did? Twenty-five thousand? Way to go, Phil! Listen. Now's not a good time to talk. What? But? [*Sighs.*] All right. Put me through. [*Listens.*] Yep. Yep. Yeah. I'm in the middle of something important here. Fine. I'll call you back.

As MICHAEL *is talking on the phone,* RON *silently gasps and flails his arms, trying unsuccessfully to catch his attention. Then he falls onto a chair, suddenly still. His eyes are open and he's sitting up, completely still.* MICHAEL *hangs up. He doesn't look at his father closely. He's too busy trying to find the words.*

Sorry about that. Dad, I'm so glad that I'm finally getting the chance to tell you how I feel. It's been... well, it's been hell, trying to be something I wasn't, and then finally admitting it to myself and *still* having to hide it. So you can imagine how... liberated I'm feeling now... but sad too... because I know this isn't the way you ever thought things would turn out. I know this is pretty hard to deal with, so just, let it sink in. Take some time. Take the rest of your life if you want, because… [*Smiles.*] God. It's so great to have you *listening* to me, giving me your full attention, not you know, interrupting, and…

Moves to RON *with the intention of hugging him.*

Dad. I know I'm not usually demonstrative, but, well… I just want you to know that—Dad? Dad, what…? You're not…? Dad? Dad?!

MICHAEL *takes a close look at his father.* RON *is dead.* MICHAEL *can't believe it. The hug turns into a stranglehold around* RON*'s neck.*

You fucking bastard!!!

MICHAEL *grabs his lifeless father and starts shaking him from the shoulders.*

[*Yelling*] You'd do *anything* not to listen to me! [*Wildly looks at clock*] It's only ten thirteen, you arrogant arsehole!

DAWN *enters, followed by* KAREN, DEBBIE *and* TED.

DAWN: Michael! Why are you screaming at your poor—(father)
MICHAEL: [*interrupting*] He's dead!

DAWN, DEBBIE, KAREN *and* TED *race over to* RON.

The bastard's dead!
KAREN: But it's only ten thirteen!
DAWN: He must be joking. [*Looks at* RON, *laughs very feebly.*] Ha ha ha ha…
MICHAEL: He's not joking. Look at this.

MICHAEL *holds one of* RON*'s arms up in the air, then drops it. It flops lifelessly.*

He's definitely carked it.
KAREN: [*to* RON] But you're not supposed to die for ten minutes! It's only ten thirteen!
DAWN: Debbie. What does your watch say?

DEBBIE *makes a dazed gesture. She doesn't speak.*

Karen? Sweetheart…?
KAREN: I'm not wearing one.
MICHAEL: My Rolex is at the jeweller.

They all turn to look at TED.

TED: Mine's no good. It's still set on Daylight Saving.
MICHAEL: You just subtract an hour, stupid! Tell us—
DAWN: [*interrupting*] Michael. There's no need for rudeness.
MICHAEL: Just tell us what your watch says.
TED: Eleven twenty-four—twenty-five.

> MICHAEL *lunges at him.*

MICHAEL: There's a ten minute difference, you stupid fucking undertaker!
KAREN: Michael! It's not Ted's—(fault)

> MICHAEL *chases* TED *around a lounge chair.*

MICHAEL: Why didn't you tell us the clock was ten minutes slow?!
TED: How do you know your clock's slow? Maybe my watch is ten minutes fast.

> MICHAEL *bails* TED *up against a wall. He grabs him by the scruff of the neck.*

MICHAEL: All right. I'm going to ring one one nine four. And if that clock is ten minutes slow, you'd better head back to your undertaker's office and come back with a hearse built for two Pal!

> MICHAEL *starts dialling 1194.*

DAWN: Michael. Don't be so mean.
KAREN: It's not his fault.

> MICHAEL *grabs* TED *by the scruff of the neck.*

MICHAEL: If the time guy says ten twenty-four, it's goodnight Irene.
KAREN: Michael, calm down!
DAWN: I'm terribly sorry about this, Ted.
TED: [*from his uncomfortable position held by the scruff of the neck*] It's all right Mrs Patterson. Different people react to the sudden death of a loved one in very different ways.
MICHAEL: [*along with time reader*] At the third stroke it will be... ten twenty-six precisely. Beep—!
TED: Don't hurt me!

> *But* MICHAEL *drops* TED *and sinks onto the floor.*

MICHAEL: ... Beep... beep...

> *He starts sobbing, as* TED *tries to get himself back in order.*

DAWN: Oh Sweetheart..

MICHAEL: I'm so tired of Dad always having the last word... [*Beat. His shoulders heave.*] He always has to have the last word.

DAWN: Oh Sweetheart...

> DAWN *instinctively moves to the sobbing* MICHAEL. *Meanwhile* DEBBIE *sits in stunned silence.*

There there...

> KAREN *moves over to* RON *and props him back up.* TED *watches helplessly.*

TED: Please let me be the first to offer my sincere condolences. Post-death, I mean.

DAWN: Thank you Ted.

TED: Ron was a very highly regarded member of the community, as well as a loving husband and father—

MICHAEL: Don't give us the spiel. You never met him before tonight.

TED: Maybe. But it only took half an hour to see that he was a truly wonderful father.

DAWN: No Ted. He wasn't a wonderful father. But he tried his heart out tonight. And that will have to be good enough for us. [*Beat.*] Now I'd like you to leave us alone with him, please.

TED: Of course. I've got some paperwork I can do in the hearse. I'll be back in a few minutes.

> DAWN *smiles.* TED *nods respectfully and exits. Left alone, they all gaze at* RON. DEBBIE *is in a daze.*

DEBBIE: I didn't believe it...

DAWN: He's gone.

DEBBIE: I didn't think he'd really die...

DAWN: I've lost my darling...

> DAWN *gently touches* RON*'s face.*

We've all lost our grumpy, silly darling.

DEBBIE: Is this... I can't believe this is happening...

> DEBBIE *looks away, then puts her head in her hands.* DAWN *walks over and puts her arms around her.*

KAREN: He looks so pale.

MICHAEL: What do you expect?

KAREN: But he looks… unhealthy.
MICHAEL: Karen. He's *dead*.
KAREN: He wouldn't want to look like that. He thought he was handsome.
DAWN: He *was* handsome. [*Beat.*] He *is* handsome.

> KAREN *quietly reaches into her handbag and gets out her cosmetics bag. As* DAWN *comforts* DEBBIE *and* MICHAEL *stares at her listlessly, she applies rouge and lipstick to her dead father's face with infinite tenderness.*

[*Stroking* DEBBIE] Ssssh… there, there Sweetheart.

> DEBBIE *cries quietly.* MICHAEL *is close to tears himself. Rather than let the pain engulf him, he's searching for reasons to still be angry.*

DEBBIE: The baby will never know him…
MICHAEL: I'm going to sue the clock company. I'm going to take them for every penny they've got.
DAWN: It was my fault Michael. I forgot to replace the batteries.
MICHAEL: It wasn't your fault. Dad did it deliberately. I bet he tampered with the clock. Just so he could have the last word.
DAWN: Now you're being silly.

> MICHAEL *starts heading towards the clock. He rips it off the wall, a maniac with a mission. He pulls it apart.*

MICHAEL: It would be just like him. All my life he's never listened to me, he's just talked at me. This is the first time he's spent five silent minutes since 1974!
KAREN: Shut up Michael!
MICHAEL: He died to spite me, I'm telling you…
KAREN: [*to* RON] Don't listen to him!

> DAWN *and* DEBBIE *look around and see* RON *wearing makeup.*

DAWN: [*touched*] Oh, Karen…
KAREN: How does he look?
DEBBIE: He looks like Joan Collins.

> *They all laugh through their tears. Sniffles all round.*

DAWN: He looks lovely.

> *They all pause and gaze at him. Then* DAWN *has an idea.*

Let's take one last family slide. At home with the Pattersons. Michael. The camera's in the top of the cabinet.

> MICHAEL *hesitates.*

DAWN: Come on Sweetheart. One last slide.

MICHAEL: What's the point? He's—

KAREN: The point is Mum wants to. And so do we.

> DEBBIE *nods and sniffles.*

DEBBIE: Come on Michael.

> *Against his better judgement* MICHAEL *moves to the cabinet and gets out the camera.*

DAWN: You know how to use the self-timer, don't you?

> MICHAEL *is setting the camera up on the edge of the table and looking through the lense.*

MICHAEL: I've got to say, I find this is a bit weird.

DAWN: [*interrupting*] What's weird about taking a family slide? Sorry Ron, what's that?

> DAWN *leans forward to listen as though* RON *were whispering to her.*

Your father says shut up and take the photo.

> *The kids look at* DAWN *in surprise. The mood changes a little and hysteria takes over.*

DEBBIE: He didn't say that.

DAWN: He did so.

DEBBIE: He can't talk Mum. [*Beat.*] He's dead as a dodo.

> *A moment's shocked silence. Then* KAREN *joins in the game.*

KAREN: He's kicked the bucket.

DAWN: He's pushing up daisies.

> *They giggle.* MICHAEL *is disapproving.*

MICHAEL: [*fiddling with the camera*] I don't believe this.

DEBBIE: [*overlapping, laughing*] He's like the parrot from Monty Python. He's ceased to be.

KAREN: You're a very dead daddy.

> *The women giggle again. Their inane giggles turn tearful.*

DAWN: [*sniffles and smiles*] Your father said to hurry up Michael.
MICHAEL: What's his rush? He's not going anywhere.

The women erupt into giggles again.

DAWN: [*to* RON] Listen to your cheeky son.
MICHAEL: [*leans over, looks through the lense*] He needs to be a bit more to the left. A bit more. Yeah. That's fine. Now Mum—

> DAWN *leans forward to listen to* MICHAEL. *The dead* RON *promptly falls behind her on the couch. Much laughter as the women prop him up again.*

... Pick him up. Yeah. That's it. Now lean in a bit... Right. Is everybody ready?

> DEBBIE *and* KAREN *nod.* DEBBIE *moves* RON's *head from side to side in a 'no' gesture. The women laugh again.*

Debbie!
DAWN: Dad's ready too.
MICHAEL: Wait. Maybe... could you make him smile?

> DEBBIE *holds up her father's lips in a smile.*

That's good—well, it'll do.
DAWN: Look at your daddy. He's happy as Larry!
MICHAEL: Okay. Here goes—

> MICHAEL *puts the self-timer on and runs into the photograph.*

DAWN: Quickly Michael!
KAREN: Quick! Over here!
DAWN: Everybody look at the camera!

> *It's a very bizarre picture of the family with the dead* RON *covered in makeup in the middle. They're all laughing.*

DEBBIE: Smile if you died five minutes ago!

> *This time—in spite of himself—*MICHAEL *laughs too. The flash and click of the camera. The shocked and laughing group breaks up.*

But then what?

> *A long silence as they all look at each other in utter futility. It's a moment of very deep sadness. Then...*

DAWN: Oh dear. Imagine if your poor father could hear us being so disrespectful.

At the front door, the distinct knocking pattern that RON *described earlier. The family stops and stares at each other in shock. An awed silence for a beat or two, then...*

The door opens and TED *enters carrying a sheet.*

TED: Just a little joke.

The reaction on their faces says all.

[*sheepish*] Wasn't... wasn't that a good idea?

Lights fade out.

We hear MICHAEL *singing in a flat and toneless voice.*

MICHAEL: What's new Pussycat? Woooo-ooh-ooooh...
What's new Pussycat? Wooo-oooh-oooh-oooh.

On the last note MICHAEL'*s toneless voice goes flat.*

THE END

Also available from Currency Press

Andrew Bovell
AFTER DINNER
An acutely observed but tender-hearted account of relationships and behaviour, *After Dinner* has been performed in Australia, New Zealand, England and Ireland. 'An Australian comedy of sharp and black social comment, full of wry insights' (Sun-Herald), the play is set in a suburban pub bistro on a Friday night where Dympie, Paula, Monika, Gordon and Stephen are all desperately seeking a good night out. Andrew Bovell is also the acclaimed author of *Lantana*, adapted for the screen from his play *Speaking in Tongues*.
ISBN 0 86819 518 9
2 Acts—2M, 3W

Elizabeth Coleman
THIS WAY UP
From the author of the box office smash hit *Secret Bridesmaids' Business* and the wonderfully dark comedy *It's My Party (And I'll Die If I Want To)* comes a funny new play about love gone wrong. Nick and Melanie's relationship is over and only boxes remain in their house—five years of shared life, sealed and marked for different addresses. Nick's workmate Damien and Melanie's sister Kris—here to load the boxes into separate cars—have brought their own emotional baggage. As life-threatening events escalate in the house next door, what was meant to be a final brief parting blows up into a riot of suppressed jealousy, insecurities and sexual tension.
ISBN 0 86819 648 7
2 Acts—2M, 3W

Ron Elisha
THE GOLDBERG VARIATIONS
A wise and witty play observing how honesty, objectivity and affection can survive the most tangled of relationships. Sol, a blind piano player, is asked by the Goldberg family to write a speech. Quick to observe the nuances of emotion that run through this family of combatants, what follows is a new life of laughter and love, with the occasional furtive tear, as he marks their births, deaths and marriages with his speeches. His vision, however, is somewhat obscured when it comes to knowledge of his own heart.
ISBN 0 86819 622 3
2 Acts—4M, 2W

Robert Hewett
WAKING EVE
A light-hearted look at suburbia and friendship, with just a touch of romance. Eve's husband was having an affair when he died prematurely and left her with a young child. Her life is falling apart, or so her friends think, but Eve's not so sure.
ISBN 0 86819 509 X
2 Acts—3M, 3W

Hannie Rayson
COMPETITIVE TENDERNESS
Hannie Rayson, the award-winning author of *Hotel Sorrento* and *Life After George*, takes a swipe at bureaucracy, corruption and romance in this very funny play. Dawn Snow has a fierce reputation—she reformed the prison system in Uganda. Now, with local government reform high on the political agenda, she is called upon to perform a similar task within the City of Greater Bourke. *Competitive Tenderness* is topical, satirical and even a little anarchic.
ISBN 0 86819 460 3
2 Acts—4M, 4W

For a full list of our titles, visit our website:

www.currency.com.au

Currency Press
The performing arts publisher
PO Box 2287
Strawberry Hills NSW 2012
Australia
enquiries@currency.com.au
Tel: (02) 9319 5877
Fax: (02) 9319 3649